## Advance Praise for *Seven Games of Life*

Master Life's Seven Games by reading, understanding, and applying these timeless principles and its perfected philosophy. —Mark Victor Hansen, coauthor of the Chicken Soup for the Soul Series

Smoley's book is a brilliant exploration of the various strategies and "games" we engage in throughout our lives, from the ordinary drive to survive to the need for love, and others. . . . One of Smoley's best.
—Ray Grasse, author of *The Waking Dream* and *When the Stars Align*

Splendidly researched, comprehensive, quite entertainingly readable, and often startling.
—John Shirley, author of *The Other End*

Whatever topic Richard Smoley tackles and investigates, he consistently delivers a thoughtful and highly readable deep dive. . . . This latest book is no exception.
—Jay Kinney, founder, *Gnosis* magazine, and author of *The Masonic Myth*

T0046672

BOOKS BY RICHARD SMOLEY

*Conscious Love: Insights from Mystical Christianity*

*The Deal: A Guide to Radical and Complete Forgiveness*

*The Dice Game of Shiva:
How Consciousness Creates the Universe*

*The Essential Nostradamus*

*First Flowering: The Best of "The Harvard Advocate,"
1866–1976* (editor)

*Forbidden Faith: The Secret History of Gnosticism*

*Hidden Wisdom: A Guide to the Western Inner Traditions*
(with Jay Kinney)

*How God Became God: What Scholars Are
Really Saying about God and the Bible*

*Inner Christianity: A Guide to the Esoteric Tradition*

*Introduction to the Occult*

*Supernatural: Writings on an Unknown History*

*A Theology of Love: Reimagining Christianity
through "A Course in Miracles"*

# SEVEN
# GAMES
## *of* LIFE
### AND HOW TO PLAY

# RICHARD SMOLEY

MEDIA

Published 2023 by Gildan Media LLC
aka G&D Media
www.GandDmedia.com

Front cover design by Tom McKeveny

Interior design by Meghan Day Healey of Story Horse, LLC.

Library of Congress Cataloging-in-Publication Data is available
upon request

ISBN: 978-1-7225-0624-7

10   9   8   7   6   5   4   3   2   1

# Contents

# Prologue
## *The Game*

From time to time you hear rumors about a game. It is said to be the ultimate game: compared to it, chess, go, and all others are no better than tic-tac-toe.

At first, you pay no particular attention; this rumor just passes through your mind like any other bit of news. But the topic comes up more than once and you learn that there really is such a game. You meet some veterans, who confirm that it surpasses all others. Some even say, "You haven't lived until you've played it."

Other details are obscure. You ask its name and are told, "It doesn't really have a name," or "You'll find out after you've played." Veterans are maddeningly vague about everything else as well.

Soon this game becomes more than a matter of curiosity to you.

You are put in contact with the organizers of the game, but their descriptions are no more specific. You are merely told that you will play for an indefinite amount of time; then you will be removed for reasons that may or may not make sense in terms of the game. Some players stay in for decades; others are removed almost immediately, for reasons that are not given. You will not be told how long you will be playing.

Nor are you told the rules or the object of the game, or even if it has any. You are told only that there will be other players. The game has been going on for a long time and will continue after you have left.

The game will take up all of your waking life. You will not be permitted to take breaks. When it is over for you, you will leave, and that is that. Nevertheless, you remain free at all times: you only have to say you want to leave and you will be immediately removed.

The organizers refuse to tell you whether the game has any rewards if played right; it may or may not. After you have finished, you will be able to evaluate the experience for yourself.

These explanations are so frustrating that you are tempted to name the game "may or may not."

"Can I get hurt?" you ask.

"Yes, you can get hurt very badly," the organizers reply. "You can endure an extraordinary amount of pain and suffering. We do, however, monitor the game very precisely, and when you reach a certain threshold of suffering, you will be immediately removed. We can assure you that you will suffer no permanent damage.

"On the other hand, it is not all about hardship and suffering. You will have the opportunity for genuine joys and rewards—all in the context of the game, of course."

The organizers tell you no more. They do not pressure you or imply any need for hurry.

You have no idea of what to do with this information. The prudent response is to walk away, at least for enough time to think. Yet spontaneously, almost before you realize it, you decide to play.

Immediately you are put into the game. About its setting, all you can say is that it is extremely confusing. It bears no resemblance to real life—so little that you are barely able to walk or move at first. The other players speak a language that you have never heard before and do not understand. The situation would be hopeless unless certain people took you in, fed you, and told you how to move around.

This process seems to take eternities. But little by little, you realize that you have a definite place in this game, determined at first by the people who took you in. If they have some status or power, it extends to you; if they are in a low situation, that extends to you as well.

As you navigate your way, you also discover that you have certain strengths and weaknesses that either enable you to function in this realm or impede you from doing so. They have no relation to your characteristics in the real world.

Some participants, you learn, are playing games within the game. One is to amass quantities of a certain object. As far as you can see, the choice of object is completely arbitrary, but it was made long before you started to play. Your share of these objects makes a great deal of difference to your game life: you soon find that you can hardly get anything to eat or even find a place to sleep without them.

At first, you find the process of obtaining these objects as mystifying as everything else in this world. But eventually, by observation and trial and error, you learn ways of acquiring them.

You may find this particular subgame easy or difficult. Obscurely you sense that your ability in it has something to do with your strengths and weaknesses as a game character. Even so, some players with great strengths and few weaknesses have very few of these objects; others with few positive qualities amass a large number. In any case, players who are taken out of the game leave all of these things behind them, which are divided among the remaining players.

Others play with sex and love. Some copulate indiscriminately, although you soon learn that this is frowned upon and usually forbidden (but by whom?). Most, however, attempt to find a partner they can stay with for the course of the game. This becomes a bitter preoccupation. Some, even most, succeed, but others fail and suffer great disappointment. Bonds, love, attachment develop. When a player's partner is pulled from the game, the player grieves, having no idea of whether they will ever meet again.

As you adapt, you are led to a certain observation: the rules that appear to enable you to succeed here do not always apply. The minute you think you understand how to achieve something, some incident or person comes along to prove otherwise.

Worst of all are disruptions that have no apparent connection to anyone's actions. People amass quantities of valuable items only to wake up the next day to find that they have vanished. Others wake up to find that they are, in the game's context, rich.

You are particularly frightened by one set of occurrences: sometimes, for no known reason, a large group of people are removed from the game. Sometimes they all live in a certain vicinity; other times, the removal has to do with some apparently irrelevant quality that they have in common: for example, all red-haired people in a given area may be taken out at once.

Some players are frustrated by these conditions. They shake their fists and curse the organizers (whom they cannot see); others beg them for help. These actions have no apparent effect.

The frustration builds to the point where people take it out on one another. Fights break out, sometimes causing serious harm. But as the organizers told you, individuals who are hurt beyond a certain point are removed from the game.

Even more frightening are the large-scale fights. Groups of people, almost all of them men, decide that another group are enemies. Sometimes a reason is given—for example, the other group has more items of value—but more often, the causes for these outbursts are inexplicable. Yet many men are injured, and many of these are removed from the game.

Other individuals try to make sense of this confusing situation. They devote a great deal of attention to figuring out the game's rules. Some claim to have succeeded: if you follow them, you too will succeed.

These individuals can be very persuasive and attract large numbers of followers. You, however, notice that the rules that these groups observe have little or no connection to the actual progress of events.

But it is dangerous to point this out to those who have faith in these rules. Often there is hostility between different groups of followers, which break out into open conflicts.

At times you are so bewildered or frightened that you want to quit. But here the same uncertainties apply: what if the object of the game is to stay until you are removed, and asking to be removed means you have lost? Indeed many of the other players insist that this is the case, although, of course, they have no more idea of the truth than you do. All learning takes place within the game and appears to have no applications outside it.

The confusion deepens because, being totally immersed in this game, you forget that there is anything else. Occasionally a shadow of a memory of your real world life passes across your mind, but it is so faint that you ignore it or decide it is just your imagination.

Your only reminder of the real world is the fact that players are removed from the game all the time. You have been told in advance that you will be removed yourself. But you have become so immersed in the game that this possibility frightens you; you have forgotten who or what you are, and even whether you exist, outside of it. Most of the other players avoid any recollection of the life beyond, and some have even ceased to believe in it.

You drift toward bizarre streams of thought. At one point, you are having lunch and are pouring blue cheese dressing onto your salad. It occurs to you: what if your success in the game is entirely determined by how much blue cheese dressing you consume? Or what if the object is to snap your fingers, and the number of times you snap your fingers is the measure of your success? Or what if there are no rules? What if the game is merely a playground to frolic on, indulging in whatever amusements the players make up?

These questions have occurred to the other players as well, and you discuss them endlessly, always ending in the same stalemate: whatever conclusions you may draw, no one knows the answers any more than anyone else.

Soon you recognize that such trains of thought are unhealthy. You decide that until you have figured out the object of the game, the best approach is to live as good a life you can while you are in it.

Those who at first appear to have the best lives are those who have amassed the largest number of possessions, but you soon realize that this has almost no actual connection with happiness. Indeed the wealthiest ones are the most anxious: somebody may take their possessions away, or they may wake up to find that everything is gone. Nor do they like the idea that when the game is over for them, all of these things will be passed on to someone else.

On further consideration, you see that the happiest people are those who have amassed enough of the goods of this life to survive, but not enough to arouse others' greed or envy. They live quietly and peaceably, enjoying good relations with those around them and having few enemies. These people are no more immune to sudden convulsions than anyone else, but they accept misfortunes with good humor, understanding that these are merely part of the game.

Some of these people seem to have gone further. Unlike the fabricators of rules, they utter some things that suggest they do have insight into the game. They avoid amassing followers, living more quietly and obscurely than anyone else. People occasionally ask them about what it all means, but their answers are unclear and even paradoxical or self-contradictory. Occasionally they will speak in a strange language that you dimly remember as the language of the real world, but although it made sense there, here it is incomprehensible. Hence most players assume that these people are insane.

Finally, you make a shocking discovery: the meaning or object of the game cannot be known within the game itself.

# Introduction

f life is a game, it is easy to believe that its object is unknown, perhaps unknowable, within the game itself.

Perhaps the universe is a game in its own right. In India, some Brahmin women play *pancikarana kattam* ("squares of quintuplication"), invented by a Tamil female saint in the eighteenth century. It depicts *lila*, "the unceasing, cosmic 'game' in which no player wins or loses, and in which all participate equally," according to writer Kanchana Natarajan.

The "quintuplication" of the name reflects the five elements described by this tradition: fire, air, water, earth, and *akasha* or ether. One phase replicates the process of creation and evolution, another the dissolution. The final emptying of the board "came as a shock," Natarajan writes, "deeply moving and unsettling, indescribably stark as well as indescribably serene. Each level of 'cosmic' embedment, from macro- to micro-level, had been taken apart as faultlessly as it had been constructed." Hindu tradition teaches that our universe undergoes this same process, like countless others in the stretches of eternity.

At any rate, both the object and the rules of life can be viewed in numberless ways. My late friend Jo-Anne Hahn, trained as an Adlerian psychologist, once worked on a dissertation at the University of Chicago on *seeming*, which she never finished and which I have never read. Seeming, she pointed out, is both passive (that person *seems* sad) and active (that person is trying to *seem* in control of the situation). Possibly the entire game of life is wrapped up in nest after nest of seeming.

It occurred to me also to speak in this book of life as a set of problems. Problems are the most mysterious yet omnipresent elements in our lives. You have a problem; you solve it; why, then, should another rise up immediately to take its place? Or why should it lead so immediately to another problem?

Often when I wake in the morning, I find myself conscious but without an identity, momentarily (and happily) unaware of who I am. Then the problems—

big, small, passing, ongoing—rush into my head to remind me. Is my identity nothing more than a conglomeration of problems?

Other systems characterize life in terms of needs, such as Abraham Maslow's famed hierarchy.

In Maslow's original system, the most basic need is survival, followed by safety, love, and esteem. These are *deficiency needs*: motivation to acquire them declines to the degree that they are satisfied: the individual then passes on to the next.

Maslow contrasted these with *growth needs*, motivation for which *increases* as they are met. In Maslow's original version of the hierarchy, self-actualization was the only growth need. According to psychologist Saul McLeod, it refers "to the realization of a person's potential, self-fulfillment, seeking personal growth and peak experiences. Maslow . . . describes this level as the desire to accomplish everything that one can, to become the most that one can be."

Later versions added other growth needs: *cognitive needs* (knowledge, understanding, curiosity), *aesthetic needs* (appreciation of beauty), and finally *transcendence needs*—for values beyond the personal self, including mystical experience, service to others, and religious faith.

Maslow's system has inspired imitators. NielsenIQ, a market analysis firm, came up with its own version:

**Protective needs:** Focused on urgent desires for safety and protection from immediate threats.

**Preservation needs:** Focused on the broad spectrum of self-care, improving current physical or emotional well-being and connections.

**Aspirational needs:** Focused on preventative care and taking proactive actions to achieve and maintain specific health goals, or helping to avoid ailments in the long term.

**Evolving needs:** Focused on innovative care solutions and seeking out the latest alternatives or developments to continuously meet health and wellness goals.

**Altruistic needs:** Focused on selfless care and improving the world around us by advocating for environmental, ethical, humanitarian and/or philanthropic causes.

Yet Maslow has his critics. Psychologist Steven Reiss argues that "an hierarchy applicable to all persons lends itself to misuse." Claiming that his findings (unlike Maslow's) are "based on scientific research," he sets out sixteen basic desires: power, independence, curiosity, acceptance, order, saving, honor, idealism, social contact, family, status, vengeance, romance, eating, physical exercise, and tranquility. Unlike Maslow's pyramid, Reiss's sixteen-slotted box consists of more or less independent and equal factors. He does not rank them.

Another perspective comes from Spiral Dynamics, a conceptual system pioneered by the late psychologist Clare W. Graves, which ranks people in terms of ᵛMEMEs (*sic*): "A ᵛMEME transposes itself into a world *view*, a *valuing* system, a *level* of psychological existence, a belief *structure*, organizing *principle*, a *way* of thinking, and a *mode* of living."

By this theory, there are eight different ᵛMEMEs, which are arranged in an upward spiral and characterized by colors. We might illustrate this system by looking at an arguably typical American family at a holiday dinner.

There's Grandma. A timid, quiet soul, she prays the rosary three times a day and has to be driven to mass each morning.

There's Dad. A retired Marine colonel, he's a midlevel manager who didn't get far in civilian life because he treats his subordinates like boot campers.

There's cousin Dave. Unemployed and unemployable. Everyone is resigned to the fact that he will be asking for money before he leaves. He is surrounded by a buffer of family hopes that he will not burst into an unexpected act of violence.

Son Phil is a high-powered salesman of an obscure but indispensable industrial part. His Jaguar flashes out from among the more humdrum vehicles in the driveway.

Mom works part-time at a local food cooperative. She spends a great deal of her free time volunteering for a habitat restoration group. She and Dad don't talk much about politics, but when they do, they argue.

Each of these figures reflects a $^V$MEME.

At the bottom is BEIGE, "underpinned by survival processes . . . automatic, autistic, reflexive." Cousin Dave.

Next is PURPLE, who obeys "desires of the mystical spirit beings" and shows "allegiance to elders, custom, clan." Grandma.

RED: "I'm tough and expect those around me to be tough or else. I take charge of people." There's Dad. Or is he BLUE—"I stand fast for what is right, proper, and good, always subjecting myself to the directives of proper authority"—as in the Marine Corps?

ORANGE: "I want to achieve, and win, and get somewhere in life. The world is full of opportunities for those who'll seize the day and take some calculated risks." Phil, who found a world of opportunities in a small industrial part.

GREEN believes in sharing society's resources among all, and believes "the community grows by synergizing life forces; artificial divisions take away from everyone." A snapshot of Mom.

Missing from this festive board are the two last types: YELLOW, who focuses on "functionality, competence, flexibility, and spontaneity" and finding a "natural mix of conflicting 'truths' and 'uncertainties.'" That could be daughter Kathy. She's not here because her job as a product developer for Apple is keeping her near company HQ.

TURQUOISE, with its "focus on the good of all living entities as integrated systems" and "expanded use of human brain/mind tools and competencies," may be represented by Steve, a relative who operates an advanced management think tank out of Santa Barbara. He talks in elaborate futuristic jargon that nobody else in the family understands.

Spiral Dynamics is a complex but elegant system for explaining human motivations, ranging from survivalist Dave to visionary Steve. These types characterize not only individuals but levels of culture, ranging from tribal levels to the present-day global mentality.

Timothy Leary, the apostle of psychedelics, took another approach, characterizing life as a game. In a predictably idiosyncratic book called *The Game of Life*, illustrated by tiny mocking caricatures of Henry Kissinger, Jimmy Carter, and Moshe Dayan (it was first published in 1979), he breaks down the human enterprise into a series of games that reflects both

Mendeleyev's periodic table of elements and the Major Arcana of the Tarot.

Leary starts with the first Tarot card, the Fool, which "portrays your floating sucking neurotechnology," says Leary. "The Fool is your baby brain still floating away in your head." He proceeds to "the Magus," which is "your infant-shark brain still biting away in your head," and then to the Empress, "your crawling-infant brain still requiring action."

The culmination reaches past the conventional twenty-two Tarot images into "the Violet Hole Card," which "portrays your neuro-technology for understanding and participating in the voyage back into the mouth of the ulti-mate [sic] intelligence."

No doubt "*The Game of Life* is not simply a book; it is an experience." All the same, it resembles systems like Maslow's and Spiral Dynamics in depicting the game of life hierarchically. The lowest level is survival (amoebalike, for Leary), going on to more elaborate social and ultimate transcendent aims.

Yet this neat ladder of needs and aims does not reflect actuality. Maslow's hierarchy of needs is like elementary school, whereby you pass on from survival in the first grade to security in the second, and so on; having mastered one, you go on to the next. The same mode of thought operates with systems like Spiral Dynamics and Leary's.

But this is not the way things are. All of these needs operate all the time: you never graduate from your needs for food, safety, and shelter. The best you can do is to make sure they are met reliably enough so that you can go on to the others.

As Reiss saw, viewing motivations in a stairstep fashion is rather clumsy. Yet Reiss's model has clumsinesses of its own: for example, his "scientific study of the human spirit" simplistically sticks all religious activities and aspirations into one of his sixteen decidedly secular boxes.

None of these models account for exceptional cases, like the ascetic who renounces all worldly goals and starves himself hoping for an experience of the divine. Here self-transcendence has trumped all the others (even, it would appear, survival), which are not only ignored but repudiated. But social scientists, like their kin in the hard sciences, are often deft at blinding themselves to contradictory evidence.

Then there are cases that are not exceptional but aberrant: a woman suffers severe deficiencies of love and esteem, so she overcompensates on the survival need and eats enough to weigh 500 pounds. Another individual sacrifices all human values of love and compassion to win glory and power. No hierarchical ladder can deal with these peculiarities except to shrug them off. But as comedian Rodney Dangerfield observed,

"The only normal people are the ones you don't know too well."

Hence the present book, which sets out life as a series of games. Certainly some hierarchy holds true even here: survival is at the bottom and the core. "A man may have many problems," says a proverb; "a man who does not have enough bread has only one."

You never graduate completely from survival concerns. For most adults, survival is inextricably linked with money: as the philosopher Jacob Needleman has observed, there are very few problems that cannot be solved with a certain amount of money. But the game far outstrips mere economics, as any billionaire wrestling with pancreatic cancer would probably say.

Some may wonder why I did not include money among the seven games I have drawn up. I could have; in fact I could have carved the game of life into an indefinite number of subgames. But I think the money game can be divided between the survival game and the power game, while also straying across the boundaries into the love game. Besides, I think people pay too much attention to money these days, displacing onto it other anxieties that they cannot handle directly (more about this later).

Most people end up playing all of the games (except perhaps the Master Game) during their lives. At the same time, the degree of time and effort devoted to them varies for many reasons, including life stages. I find pop music enjoyable partly because it is fundamentally adolescent in outlook: young people desperately trying to find love in the form of a mate. It is not a problem that I consider myself to have anymore, so I can take some satisfaction in looking back on that game from a complacent distance as well as enjoying the effervescent energy.

What happens when the mating problem is solved? The love game isn't over. In fact, when I got married and we were having our first baby, my father-in-law portentously said, "Now it begins." I could hardly come up with another statement so concise and correct. So I play the survival game still, and play the love game as well, although in different forms than when I was single.

In fact, all the games run into and overlap one another: the survival game often means taking risks, and even risks that are not life-threatening often put one into the courage game. The courage game, taken to its height, puts one into the realm of the Master Game. Love and power have a great deal to do with each other.

There are no rigid boundaries here: I am only setting them out rather arbitrarily so that we can look at them one at a time without too much confusion. As Aristotle wrote, "The discussion can be said to be adequate if it is clear to the extent that the material under discussion allows; for precision is not to be sought to the same degree in all discourses."

The subtitle of this book—*and How to Play*—may give the misleading impression that it is a self-help title, with the usual array of instructions. These books always seem to involve making huge numbers of lists and telling the reader to get up at some ridiculously early hour in the morning.

I don't want to write another book of this kind: I do not regard it as a kindness to give anyone yet another list of things to do, and getting up at six in the morning is not something that my conscience permits me to advocate.

If I mean anything by saying "how to play," it is rather a matter of attitude—realizing that although these games may be serious up to a point, it is ruinous to take them seriously in an absolute sense. They are best played with a lightness of spirit, with the realization that losses and gains are equally temporary and that the games themselves (perhaps excepting the Master Game) are of no absolute value.

This is not, on the other hand, an encouragement to despair or apathy: we have all bought the ticket to the amusement park that is life, and we may as well take the ride.

# 1

# Survival

My late psychiatrist Jack Downing once told me about a man he knew whose concept of the ideal vacation was odd. He wanted to be dropped off in the midst of Death Valley, equipped with only a knife and a canteen of water, and picked up a week later.

This is an extreme version of the survival game.

Another example: a college friend got an internship at a major investment bank. Originally it was supposed to be a year, until he went to Harvard Law School, but he decided that he liked the work and wanted to stay on. His employers told him, "You can sink or swim with the rest of them."

My friend was successful, as, we can imagine, was the Death Valley trekker. A less happy outcome occurred for a "Traveller" in France a few years ago. "Traveller" (complete with British spelling) was the way he was described by philosopher Didier Fassin, who wrote a book about his case: *Death of a Traveller*. "Travellers" in this sense are otherwise known as Gypsies or Roma.

This particular Traveller, Angelo, had a long history of crimes, involving thefts of various sizes, none of them violent. He was not considered dangerous; in fact, the prison granted him home leave. But he did not want to go back, so he hid out in his parents' house. The GIGN (a heavily armed elite French SWAT team) swooped in, and on discovering him, immediately gunned him down.

This case, apart from telling us that police brutality is not a specialty exclusive to the United States, shows how someone can fail the survival game. The dénouement was hardly surprising in the wake of Angelo's past. As Fassin suggests, he may even have preferred it to going back to prison.

But it is the life of Angelo that shows how one fails the survival game. Initially, there were the usual sequences of crimes, arrests, and prison sentences: the

French authorities are not lenient toward the Roma. But there was one interlude:

> A more stable period follows his release two years later. He has a new girlfriend who is not a Traveller.... She gives him strong encouragement to change his way of life. He takes a course in vine-pruning in viticulture school. Both work in vineyards in the region.... Certificates from his employers testify to his qualities as a committed, reliable worker with a sense of initiative.... He is interested in what goes on in the world, in environmental issues, in politics. A brief happy interval in his adult life....
>
> But financial difficulties soon catch up with him. Court costs, old fines, financial compensation to civil parties, the child support deducted at source from his income. His meager wages go on repaying his accumulated debts. The sums due seem enormous. He says his life is shot. He has the feeling that he is being pushed down just when he was beginning to pull himself up. And he plunges in again. Takes part in robberies. Is caught. Returns to jail on remand.

With the grim outcome that followed.

People may take a complacent joy in denouncing this social injustice. But the survival game assumes that such inequities exist: at any rate, there are few if any societies without them. Survival involves managing these inequalities as deftly as possible, wherever in the social rigging we may find ourselves. We may envy those who take advantage of their privileged position, but only the most fervent self-deceivers would deny that they would do the same thing in the same circumstances.

In any event, people differ enormously in what they regard as survival. A wealthy young friend in prep school told me, "I can't imagine how anyone lives on less than $100,000 a year" (in 1974 dollars). Undoubtedly—a luxury once enjoyed becomes a necessity, especially when you have been born to it.

On the other end are the people who live under the streets of Las Vegas. The desert playland, prone to sudden rainstorms and flash floods, has built a maze of tunnels hundreds of miles in length to contain them. They range in height from four or five feet to fifteen feet or more. Journalist Michael J. Mooney writes:

For hundreds of people, these tunnels are home. These are America's forgotten, those left behind in a country with an ever-growing gap between the haves and the have nots. Some are transient—temporary occupants moving in and out every few weeks. But several tunnels have become small, off-the-map communities. There's no fresh water, and the only electricity comes from batteries, but people have still managed to piece together meager, ersatz apartments inside the industrial-sized concrete-walled waterways. Some have lived down here for a decade or more. Each occupied tunnel has its own customs and rituals and unofficial leaders. . . .

Nearly everyone in the tunnel lives with some sort of addiction, but many have also gathered enough discarded items from above to carve out some semblance of a home. They have beds with bed frames, coolers and bicycles and barbecue grills—all pulled from curbs or dumpsters. A lot of the beds and bookcases site on homemade stilts a foot or two off the ground, because when water comes through, it comes fast and hard, and sometimes it sweeps away everything it touches.

It is easy to blame addictions, but where did these addictions come from? Practically all of the drugs that are major sources of addiction—alcohol, cocaine, opioids—are analgesics. What pain are they trying to mute?

The life of bare survival goes back to the earliest times. For a picture from the nineteenth century, we can turn to Jack Black's classic memoir of 1926: *You Can't Win.*

Black was a man of superior intelligence and ability. He could easily have found a place for himself in burgeoning Gilded Age America, but he chose otherwise. He was not essentially a victim, and he was not abused: he has fond memories of his mother, who died when he was ten, after which his father sent him to a convent school, where he was treated with kindness.

Black had to leave the school when he turned fourteen, and that began his journey into the netherworld of American tramps, bums, and hoboes (each term had its specific meaning in that day). Two themes emerge from Black's memoir, which has kept its power for nearly a century. The first is his distrust of a corrupt system.

Soon after leaving school, he is working honorably, collecting bills for a local merchant when he is scooped up in a police raid on a whorehouse. A customer has complained that one of the girls stole $100 from him, and the police round everyone up and bring them to the station. A search of all the girls, and the madam, reveal nothing. The madam's lawyer shows up.

The customer is insistent. Finally, the police captain tells him to inspect his own clothes. He goes through his pockets and finds his two $50 bills. The captain turns him out rudely.

Mystifyingly, the young Black is the only one detained. He is given a cellmate, who explains it all to him:

> That's everyday business here. . . . Usually the sucker is a married man and can't squawk. But when he does squawk, like this one, the only thing to do is blow back his money. Either the lawyer or one of the girls eased it into his back pocket. That's better than returning it to him and admitting that they tried to rob him.
>
> The whole thing was a stand-in from the captain down. Everybody's satisfied. The sucker has his money, the girls are all out. . . .
>
> You appear to be the only real sucker in the bunch.

Eventually, Black is released. But his sense of a corrupt system joins up with his wanderlust, and although he has a decent job, he soon decides to drop it and go on the road.

Black prefers the rough honesty of the criminal underworld to the hypocrisy of conventional life. Even in the underworld, there is a morality: the honorable bums and thieves versus the ones who cannot be trusted—in the argot of the era, the "Johnson family" versus the "shits": the Johnsons are "good people": they pay their debts, they mind their business, but they will help when asked.

Novelist William S. Burroughs was captivated by this dichotomy and made it a central theme of his work. In a foreword to *You Can't Win*, he writes: "A basic split between shits and Johnsons has emerged. . . . Of course, any Johnson does do shitty things at times. But he knows enough to regret such actions. It is very rare that a hardcore shit acts like a Johnson. He simply does not understand what it means to be a Johnson, and is irrevocably committed to the other viewpoint."

In any event, Black is not exactly victimized by society, though he believes he is (as we see from his book's title). Throughout the narrative, there is the chance of going straight: of taking his stash of money, sometimes small, sometimes large, usually ill-gained, and setting himself in a stable life. But he does not have the appetite for it.

A helpful afterword to my edition of *You Can't Win* supplies some details about the author that he did not choose to share: "In the months before the 1906 earthquake Black was apparently a one-man reign of terror until he was caught for shooting a man in a botched holdup in Golden Gate Park and got his twenty-five year sentence."

Eventually Black was befriended by the philanthropist Fremont Older, who secured an early release for him and gave him a job at his newspaper, *The San Francisco Bulletin*. Black published *You Just Can't Win* to acclaim and later went on the lecture circuit advocating for prison reform.

In the end, Black appears to have ended where he began. His earnings dwindled with the Depression, and he disappeared in 1932. "He had once told his friends that if life got too grim he would tie weights to his feet, row out into New York harbor, and drop overboard. This seems to be precisely what he did."

Jack Black's story leads us to believe that he was playing the survival game in its purest form. He knows that the system of law and convention is skewed and hypocritical, and prefers the frank crookedness of the criminal world.

Angelo the Traveller and the subterranean citizens of Las Vegas are also playing the survival game in a crude, direct way, yet they seem more ill-fated than Jack Black: they see no alternatives for themselves, and fate chops them up. Black, more intelligent and capable, appears to have had the choice to make his decisions. Were they conscious ones (such as an existentialist might make), or were they playing out unconscious beliefs that that was the way the world was and that he could not do otherwise? Did he simply find the vagrant's life more enjoyable than middle-class stability? Burroughs did: "Stultified and confined by middle-class St. Louis mores, I was fascinated by this glimpse of an underworld of seedy rooming-houses, pool parlors, cat houses and opium dens, of bull pens and cat burglars and hobo jungles."

We will never know: we can only look into our lives and try to answer these questions for ourselves. We face them with all of the seven games, never entirely sure whether we are choosing what we want or what we think must be.

All of the cases discussed above can be seen as cases of the survival game played more or less on its own. "I had very few glasses of wine as I traveled this route," writes Jack Black. "I rarely saw a woman smile and rarely heard a song."

Not entirely: Black makes friends along the way, and even the subterranean world beneath Las Vegas has communities. Sometimes love shines its face upon this world: once, in San Francisco's Haight-Ashbury district, I saw two street people, a man and a woman, sitting on a low wall and making out. And why shouldn't they?

Even so, one must assume that the homeless population in the United States (an estimated 553,000 in 2021) is preoccupied more or less exclusively with survival. And the 42.5 million Americans who live below the poverty line (as of 2021) must have the matter constantly at the front of their minds.

Some theorists imagine that Stone Age humans, as well as present-day primitive tribes, were purely involved in the survival game. I do not believe this. We know so little about our prehistoric ancestors that much of what we posit about them is little more than speculation mixed with projection. As for primitive peoples in Africa and South America, I believe that they play the full gamut of seven games—including the Master Game—although their versions may not be recognizable as such to us. People in all societies play the seven games, whether they are Bushmen or titled British aristocrats.

Some have wondered whether a Bushman dropped onto Manhattan Island would be able to survive. At the outset, he could probably survive quite well, making a rich living trapping pigeons, rats, and squirrels, fat and lazy for want of other predators. Eventually, of course, he would attract the attentions of the police. They would see he was no criminal, but would consign him to the machinery of the social welfare system. Let us draw the curtain of charity over what would ensue.

For practically everyone, survival is not a matter of mere sustenance; it is a matter of living in a particular context—a location, a job, a family, a social and personal identity—and if it is impossible to make a go of it there, one's survival feels threatened.

What counts as survival varies wildly from individual to individual. Over thirty years ago, I was in extreme circumstances: I had lost my job, and my house was facing foreclosure. Yet all throughout that time, I continued to have my shirts laundered and have my lawn mowed, at a cost of $20 a week. Many men mow their own lawns as a matter of course, but I never have (or rather, I have tried it once or twice, but in the end have decided to leave it in the hands of professionals). In any event, keeping my lawn mown was a necessity if I wanted the house to sell (which it did, at the last minute).

Already we are far from bare-bones survival. Necessity lies in the eye of the beholder: my rich friend at prep school certainly regarded many things as necessities that most people would never imagine enjoying at all. Survival is not merely a matter of calories and shelter. It is bound up with self-image.

Consequently, the survival game can take on strange and distorted forms. Recently I chanced to read Anthony Trollope's 1865 novel *Can You Forgive Her?* and watch the *Downton Abbey* TV series at roughly the same time. Both portray a very specific version of the game. Here we are dealing with the British upper class, so it is hardly a matter of where one's next meal will come from. These works portray survival as having access to enough money to live like a lady or gentleman without having to work. The amounts vary with the characters' tastes and circumstances, but they are far above what the ordinary English person had to live on—even while working. Failure to get your hands on a fortune of this size is losing the game. The characters regard this goal as a matter of life-and-death survival.

In Trollope's novel, the erratic George Vavasor has trouble settling down into life. At one point,

> He had become a partner in an established firm of wine merchants. . . .
>
> In this employment he remained for another period of five years, and he was supposed by all his friends to be doing very well. And indeed he did not do badly, only that he did not do well enough to satisfy himself. He was ambitious of making the house to which he belonged the first house in the trade in London, and scared his partners by the boldness and extent of his views. . . . At the end of the five years Vavasor had left the house, . . . taking with him a very nice sum of money.

For George, even being a successful London wine merchant is losing the game. He is heir to a large estate, but he is estranged from his father, "a strong man of forty, with as much promise of life in him as his son had. A profession had therefore been absolutely necessary to him." George wants to go into Parliament, but this goal is remote unless he can first get his hands on a fortune.

In *Downton Abbey*, the game is essentially the same: the family must have enough money to maintain their large and costly estate, an aim that is hampered by the disruptions of the First World War. The head of the family, the Earl of Grantham, tries to navigate these waters, but not successfully: he makes bad investments, and the family faces the stark need to bring in another substantial income by marriage.

I choose these two works only because I encountered them at more or less the same time: I could point to endless other examples in British fiction from the eighteenth century on. Certainly Jane Austen's novels can be understood almost completely in this light.

Survival in the world of the British gentry is not merely accomplished with a steady 2,000 calories a day and a roof overhead: the characters have to survive, not in some rudimentary sense, but as ladies and gentlemen. Men can go into certain professions while retaining their respectability (law, the clergy, even selling wine), but women can only attain this goal by marriage (assuming, of course, that they do not carry large fortunes of their own, in which case their role in the game is quite different).

In today's United States, the game is practically the opposite. Even individuals who have never spent a second of their lives without privilege pretend, sometimes absurdly, that they are self-made. Wealthy businesspeople routinely boast about the bankruptcies they have suffered before gaining success.

Britain mixed, and mixes, a modern postindustrial civilization with quasi-feudal relics. The British make it work; only the British could make it work. In this country, the ideal is Emerson's self-reliance—the poorer, the dirtier your background, the more you can puff yourself up on your success. This usually ends up sounding vulgar and ludicrous, but that is not seen as a problem.

By now it should be obvious that I am not writing a manual on the survival game (or any of the others discussed here). The answer too should be obvious: How do you play the game? Who are you? An Ethiopian coffee grower? An industrial worker in a midsized Chinese city? A novice stockbroker trying to assemble clients?

Neither I nor anyone else has the knowledge to give specific advice in all of these circumstances, especially since it is an issue not only of technical know-how but social sophistication—always in your own context, of course. Most people, even extremely clever ones, usually manage to master only one milieu in a lifetime.

I recently downloaded a booklet entitled "Eleven Things Every Child Must Know about Money (before Leaving Home)." The advice is succinct and useful, discussing "how to open and manage accounts," "how to be a savvy shopper," and "the dire need of an emergency fund." Still, these are only the basics: the rest is acquired through long and hard experience. Even intelligent and educated Americans often feel stymied when climbing the rigging of a government agency or their health insurance plans. I wonder what a similar book in Pakistan or Saudi Arabia would have to cover. Note too that a booklet for someone approaching retirement would have to cover very different things.

Then there are the losers. The cynics remind us: "Life is a terminal disease"; "in the long run, we're all dead." Of course, but there are differences. One woman dies peacefully and painlessly in old age, surrounded by the prayers and affection of her loved ones. Others, like Angelo the Traveller, don't fare so well.

A woman was recently found wandering about the streets of Eau Claire with a dead baby in her arms. She was from Chippewa County and had lost her husband and was destitute. . . .

The sixty year old wife of a farmer in Jackson, Washington County, killed herself by cutting her throat with a sheep shears. . . .

Jerry Murphy, a chopper employed in Herrick's camp near Minocqua, was killed by the Northwestern Limited. . . . The engineer noticed him on the track, standing with his arms extended and facing toward the approaching train. The engineer could not stop the train before the man was struck. . . .

Mary Karban, wife of Wenzel Karban, a farmer of the town of Neva, committed suicide by eating the heads of four boxes of matches. She was only sixteen years old and had been married last fall.

These stories are all from Michael Lesy's cult classic *Wisconsin Death Trip*, which largely consists of newspaper snippets from Black River Falls, Wisconsin, between 1885 and 1900, providing a sharp but by no means cheerful account of life in that time and place. People all over the world have lost the survival game in ways even more pathetic and grotesque. A friend of mine came across a two-inch newspaper clipping from 1904, with the matter-of-fact headline "Boy Shooting at Rats Kills Aged Negro."

The secular Calvinists preaching the gospel of prosperity will no doubt say these sad cases failed to learn the seven habits of highly successful people or settle on the Definite Major Purpose recommended in Napoleon Hill's *Path to Personal Power*. Too bad for them.

Makers of millions can say such things. Personally, I would not want to turn my self-congratulation into contempt for my fellow humans. Besides, as Sophocles reminds us, "Never deem any mortal happy until he reaches the limit of his life without suffering grief."

As I write this at the end of 2021, it seems impossible to finish this chapter without mentioning the coronavirus pandemic. Probably only the most risk-averse have followed the precautions down to the last jot; even so, it is strange to see them so fastidiously flouted by such a large part of the population, who seem to be playing the survival game in reverse.

Disinformation and the coaxings of insane politicians only go so far toward explaining this phenomenon. So do understandable doubts fueled by the ambiguous and contradictory statements of public health officials. Much of this behavior can no doubt be chalked up to the august capacity of the human mind for denial. Perhaps *Beyond the Pleasure Principle*, one of Freud's most speculative works, takes us a little further. Here he posited the death principle—the opposite of the principle that strives to maintain life. It is, he said, the organism's desire "to return to the inanimate state." He added, "We shall be compelled to say that '*the aim of all life is death*.'"

Freud's hypothesis is daring, but still seems incomplete. I am inclined to turn to something still more mysterious: collective madness. As the late Harvard psychiatrist John Mack pointed out, the mental health discipline pays almost no attention to this subject. Yet it must be reckoned as one of the great motivators of human behavior and indeed human history.

The only theorist I know of who attempted to explore collective madness in a complete way was the Russian psychologist V.M. Bekhterev, who was able to view many instances of it firsthand during the Russian Revolution. He advances some theories in his book *Collective Reflexology*, published in the 1920s. He quotes one source, G. LeBon, in *Psychology of Nations and Masses*:

> Heroism, valor, and kindness can be characteristic of an individual person; but they can never, or hardly ever, appear as the distinguishing features of a large gathering.... A crowd is a substratum in which the germ of evil spreads very easily, while the germ of good nearly always dies for lack of the necessary conditions for survival.

Bekhterev's theories, which regard such responses as instances of "collective reflexes," are in need of amendment and amplification, but I doubt that much progress has made since his time.

*   *   *

When I was a boy, one of the charms of playing Monopoly was selecting one of the metal tokens that would represent you as the player. One was a ship (which I usually chose); others were a top hat, a Scottie dog, a flatiron, and a cannon.

Playing the survival game also requires a token, and these vary far more in appearance than the Monopoly pieces. Here the token is your body, and the game is to preserve it at all costs, as if your life depended on it—because it does. We often act as if we believe that we consist of nothing apart from this token, and that its loss is an absolute loss. The world's wisdom traditions insist on the exact opposite, but most people playing for survival do not pay much heed to them.

# 2

# Love

Survival: some, like Thomas Hobbes, regard it as a game once played individually: everyone for themselves in the brutish state of nature. But no evidence says that it has ever been that way. Archaeology shows that people have lived closely together for as far back as the record of bones and flaked stones can tell us. This means human relations, and this means love.

What is love? I will attempt a definition: *love is what unites self and other, while preserving the integrity of each.* After all, there are forms of love that do not wish to preserve the integrity of the other. The lion loves the lamb so much that it wants to eat it.

By my definition, love runs the whole gamut: it is what binds two people in whatever relation, in whatever sense. We could divide love into two categories: *conditional* and *unconditional love.* Conditional love encompasses the vast bulk of what we regard as human relations, often including those seen as unconditional. A missionary imagines that bringing the Gospel to savages is an act of unconditional love. Claude Lévi-Strauss saw through this pretense:

> Members [of the American Protestant missions in Brazil] were of a peculiar kind: their members came from Nebraska or Dakota farming families, in which young people were brought up to believe in the reality of Hell with cauldrons of boiling oil. For some, becoming a missionary was like taking out an insurance policy. Once they were certain of their own salvation, they thought there was nothing more they need do to prove themselves worthy of it, so that in the practice of their profession they displayed shocking callousness and lack of feeling.

In 2008, I published *Conscious Love: Insights from Mystical Christianity.* Since then, I have modified my views somewhat, although not substantially. In that book, I contrasted *transactional love* with *unconditional love*. At this point, I think it would be more apt to speak of *conditional* rather than *transactional* love. After all, we do not intuitively connect transaction with love. Hiring someone to do a job or selling someone an insurance policy is not in itself a loving act.

In any case, conditional love is more pervasive than it may appear. A couple falls in love. They are sure that their love is unconditional: it will never change, whatever the future brings. "No matter how it works out, I just want what's best for her."

Six weeks later, they have broken up and are wishing each other every manner of evil. We can hardly take this love as unconditional.

People often tout a mother's love as the most sublime example of the unconditional variety, but this does not hold up. In the first place, the love is completely contingent on the child being *her* child, whether adopted or begotten in the usual fashion. Many people have sacrificed their lives for their children; far fewer have made the same sacrifice for other people's children.

In the second place, parental love is usually bound up with all sorts of expectations of what the child should be or become, a fact that has provided much income for therapists. The children in turn pass on their own expectations, either taken wholesale from the parents or modified, to their own offspring. In the

Bible, the Lord says he will visit "the iniquity of the fathers upon the children unto the third and fourth generation" (Exodus 20:5). It would be more accurate to say that the fathers themselves visit their iniquities upon the children.

The most obvious aspect of the love game has to do with mating. We can look at this process at all stages, which frequently follow upon one another rapidly and often automatically. A man sees a bewitching pair of eyes across a crowded room; the next thing he knows, she is driving the kids to soccer in a Disney World sweatshirt.

Most people believe that happiness in this world depends upon finding a lifelong mate; whether that is a person of the opposite sex, the same sex, or somewhere in between is a mere technicality. At some point, the couple usually formalize their bond in marriage.

Not everyone does marry, and not everyone wants to. The percentage of never-married people in the United States has increased from 9 percent in 1970 to 35 percent in 2018, partly because living together unmarried is much less stigmatized than in the past. Finding a lifelong mate no longer automatically means marriage, but the mating game still appears to be a central goal for most people.

Whether played for the long, short, or intermediate term, the mating game is based on the Equation.

You know what the Equation is; everyone does. It is a calculation of the ostensible value of one individual compared to another. You know what the Equation is if you have ever said, "She could do better than him," or if you even know what this means.

World literature offers innumerable examples. In Thomas Hardy's *Return of the Native*, the two-timing Wildeve is engaged to Thomasin Yeobright, a farmer's daughter, but the marriage is interrupted by an irregularity in the license. All is thrown in doubt, because Wildeve is secretly in love with the genteel Eustacia Vye. As he dithers about his decision, Thomasin's mother comes to him saying that another man has asked for her daughter's hand. Wildeve, at loss for what to do, goes to Eustacia and tells her this. Her response:

> What curious feeling was this coming over her? Was it really possible that her interest in Wildeve had been so entirely the result of antagonism that the glory and the dream departed from the man with the first sound that he was no longer coveted by her rival? She was, then, secure of him at last. Thomasin no longer required him. What a humiliating victory! He loved her best, she thought; and yet—dared she to murmur such treacherous criticism ever so softly?—what was the man worth whom a woman

inferior to herself did not value? The sentiment which lurks more or less in all animate nature—that of not desiring the undesired of others—was lively as a passion in the supersubtle, epicurean heart of Eustacia. Her social superiority over him, which hitherto had scarcely ever impressed her, became unpleasantly insistent, and for the first time she felt that she had stooped in loving him.

Here, as in much of British fiction, social class is at the forefront. But value lies in a number of other elements as well: beauty, youth, health, intelligence, character, a sense of humor, and money are the most prominent.

The game of romantic love is played using the Equation. The individual calculates the value of a prospective partner in relation to their understanding of their own. Often men will say or think, "She's out of my league"—usually meaning that the woman is far more attractive than he believes himself to be. Of course no one reckons their own value objectively or entirely correctly. But on the whole, the Equation works out more or less as you would expect. Beautiful women marry handsome men. Smart men marry smart women. Partners are generally the most comfortable when they come from more or less the same social class. (Note how Eustacia's "social superiority" to Wildeve "became unpleasantly insistent" to her.)

What happens when one partner is of much higher value (as perceived by the people themselves and/or by the culture at large)? As long as both people are happy, nothing. The one of supposedly lower value is grateful for the luck. But discrepancies of value can lead the superior party to regret, and in the worst cases, to bitterness, recrimination, abuse, and desertion. Of the countless examples in literature, we can pick the marriage of Flaubert's beautiful and ambitious Emma Bovary to a lackluster country doctor. The story, of course, ends in tragedy.

Abundance of one factor may supersede deficiencies in others, as we see with bald, shrimpy billionaires with statuesque wives. I do not know why Marilyn Monroe married Arthur Miller, although it was probably more for his brilliance than his good looks. I have been told that an uncle of mine married his wife because she had large breasts. Some people give heavy weight to money. (One proverb says if you marry for money, you will earn it.) For others, it is a resemblance to a beloved celebrity or an eighth-grade crush, a certain style or flair, or anything that the French file under the rubric of *je ne sais quoi*.

Occasionally one quality trumps all others. Years ago, I had a girlfriend who was divorced. She told me that years before, she had been very nervous when she was about to meet her future husband's family. He told her, "I could have dragged you in off the street as long as you were Jewish." She was, so the parents approved, although the marriage did not last. I gathered that the husband's family learned their lesson and did not object to his marriage to a non-Jewish woman the second time around.

Many women today are preoccupied with body image, worrying they are too fat or too thin, their breasts are too small or their noses too large.

"Body image influences our daily thoughts more than it should," writes Shirley Ojeda in an op-ed piece. Ashamed of her weight (380 pounds at a maximum), Ojeda Photoshopped the photos of her that she posted on social outlets. She writes:

> Looking back at all the Photoshopped images, it's impossible not to feel a sense of regret. I know that the photos I see are fake, so why did I try to edit my body image with Photoshop? Why was I so afraid and embarrassed of my body curvature? More than once, I've found myself wondering these questions, and the answer is because I tied my inner beauty, my true self-value, to my weight.

She adds, "The size of your body has nothing to do with your beauty, but I thought if I was not comfortable with my mirror's reflection, as well as with my health, then I should act upon it." Ojeda went on a weight-loss program and reduced to 220 pounds, part-way to her goal of 160 pounds.

However reinforced by glamour magazines and fashion catwalks, such fears are mostly delusory, at least as far as they are concerned with desire by the opposite sex. I would suggest that any woman obsessed with body image visit a porn website. There she will see, in lurid detail, women of all shapes and sizes— white, Asian, black, Hispanic, skinny, obese, young, middle-aged, elderly. There is no possible variation that does not appear. This woman should also remem-ber that no one is sitting at home masturbating to these videos in order to prove they are body-positive: someone somewhere is genuinely, even furtively, aroused by them. This ought to dispel anxieties about conforming to some fictitious ideal that can never be reached anyway.

I feel no need to give any such reassurance to men, since many American males do not seem to give any attention to their appearance whatsoever.

The Equation, a concept I devised and discussed in my book *Conscious Love*, explains a great deal. But it cannot account for everything. Beyond is the elusive matter of *type*.

Everybody knows this term. They often use it in a street-level sense, physically or culturally. If a woman says a man is "not her type," she probably means that he is too macho, or not macho enough, for her. A Goth might not look for love outside of the circle of Goths. But the power of types reaches much further. The spiritual teacher G.I. Gurdjieff told his pupils, "Each of you . . . has probably met in life people of one and the same type. Such people often even look like one another, and their inner reactions to things are exactly the same. What one likes the other will like. What one does not like the other will not like."

A student asks, "How many fundamental types are there in all?"

"Some people say twelve. . . . According to the legend the twelve apostles represented the twelve types. Others say more."

Gurdjieff does not elaborate, but someone could pull together an encyclopedia of types, among them the enneagram, the Myers-Briggs type indicator, and William Sheldon's body types. But the system best known in this culture is the astrological one. (The twelve apostles have also been correlated with the twelve signs of the zodiac.)

The learned sneer at astrology as if it were worth the attention of no one more sophisticated than the typical fifteen-year-old girl. Nevertheless, in my experience it works as well, or better, than any of the modern psychological methods for determining both character and compatibility. The basics are widely known. You want a mate with a sun sign in the same element, or the complementary one, to your own. Water signs go best with other water signs, along with earth signs. Fire and air signs pair up the same way. Although this does not always apply, I have had enough experience with this myself to take it seriously.

Astrology goes much further than sun signs. It is a complex discipline that often reveals traits and affinities in a way that seems uncanny. The tradition holds that marital compatibility is at its best when the man's sun (or ascendant) is conjunct the woman's moon. The Swiss psychiatrist C.G. Jung did a study of the astrological charts of married couples to test this belief, and to some extent verified it. The percentage of married couples with these and similar aspects was higher than for any other aspects.

Many other factors in astrological charts complicate these simple principles. Nevertheless, astrology holds out more promise for determining compatibility than any other system I know.

However you cast it, type is a major key to romantic fulfillment.

In any event, most people give marriage or its modern surrogate—monogamous cohabitation—a try at some point. How do you define success in this context? Mental health and stability for both parties? The way the kids turned out? The longevity of the relationship? The elusive bluebird of happiness?

Many, perhaps most, marriages end happily in the long run. Others do not. In one variant, two people may love each other, but a stint at domestic life reveals their incompatibility. In another, one partner falls prey to infidelity—to the other, the unforgivable sin. Alcoholism, drug addiction, abuse, and financial ruin offer other variations. So does plain old selfishness. Steven Reiss's principle applies to many cases: "Couples bond when their desire profiles are similar. . . . Couples grow apart when their desire profiles are dissimilar," or when they change. Two status- and money-hungry people get married at age twenty-five. One stays the same, but twenty years later, the other decides that these satisfactions are hollow. They will probably separate.

Most striking are the cases when two elderly people separate having been married for decades. Probably they have simply gotten tired of each other. In Iain Reid's novel *I'm Thinking of Ending Things*, one character says: "Most relationships I've been in were like a carton of milk reaching its expiration date. It gets to a certain point and sours, not inducing sickness but enough to notice a change in flavor."

For the most part, I would say that when a marriage collapses, the partners may divide up the property however they like, but the blame is to be allocated on a 50-50 basis.

As I have said, the games bleed into one another, nowhere as profoundly and mysteriously as in the juncture between the survival game and the mating game. I have often wondered: a cell divides into two. What relation do these two cells have to the first? Is one the parent, which thereby achieves a kind of immortality? Are both of the new cells offspring of the parent, which has now ceased to exist?

Sexual reproduction leaves no such questions. The offspring are definitely separate organisms. Because they blend two sets of genes, they do not resemble either parent completely. Individuals do survive in their offspring, but in what way? This question, abstract when stated here, becomes concrete and often confusing in real life. How much should the son be a chip off the old block? In the past, the answers were clear: the son would take on the same occupation as the father. He would live in the same family and in the same village, which had specific customs and traditions and property. We have already seen how for Downton Abbey's Earl of Grantham, the futures of the family and the estate are inextricable.

Today the values are almost the opposite. Current social expectations—expressed in nearly every movie made in the past generation—say that the child should find his or her own way to achieve Maslow's self-actualization, even in the face of parental opposition. As mythologist Joseph Campbell famously said, "Follow your bliss." Instead of being one link in a long chain of ancestry and heritage, the family is an obstacle to overcome.

I won't rail against the confusion and uncertainty created by the new values, or vice versa. I am simply making what I believe to be objective observations. No doubt the ancient tradition of family continuity had its advantages and drawbacks, as does the current urge toward reversal and revolt.

In the end, few if any things in ordinary existence give such real, heartfelt, and enduring joys as a happy family life. A happy childhood is no small gift, and the parent often takes the same satisfaction in a healthy, successful adult child that an artist does in creating a masterwork. I would not want guess which of the two is the harder job. And certainly parents are judged heavily on the outcome. In the Old Testament, the worthless sons of Aaron and Eli point to their fathers' inner weakness.

Yet the paradoxes inherent in living as a human are never so acute as they are with family, producing pains and crimes that can be found nowhere else. The Greek tale of Uranus devouring his children, horrifically portrayed by Goya, is more than a mere myth. Look at the great tragedies of Western civilization: the *Oresteia*, *Antigone*, *Oedipus Rex*, *Hamlet*, *King Lear*. All of them center around treachery and hurt in families, sometimes inadvertent (as in *Oedipus Rex*), sometimes well thought out (*Hamlet*). *Lear* is powerful in part because the wicked daughters are in their way justified by the old man's obnoxious behavior in their homes. The Compson family in Faulkner's novels is haunted by a hereditary guilt that seems to prevail among certain old Southern families—although *The House of the Seven Gables* shows something similar among the old families of New England. On a more contemporary note, *The Godfather* tells about the burden of hereditary crime. Common wisdom is right in judging the parents by how the children turn out.

In the end, I stand by what I said in *Conscious Love*: family love is powerful, overwhelming, and all-encompassing, but it cannot be called unconditional. It can only be made unconditional by acknowledging the backdrop of conditions against which it is set.

Friendship has been lavishly praised, from Aristotle and Epicurus to rows of cards in Hallmark shops. Yet few seem to realize that it is the most important of all human relationships.

Romance. Marriage. Family. Many people regard these as having supreme value. Yet tens of millions of people live full, happy, successful lives without lovers, spouses, or families. Some have actively turned their backs on this dimension of life.

Yet practically no one lives or can live a happy life without friends. Even a married man with an established family but without any outside friends will often be psychologically unstable.

Friendship is a freer relationship than romantic or family love. Demands and expectations are lower. There is no jealous eye to exclusive possession (at least not in healthy friendships). At its core, its joys are in companionship—shared activities, shared outlooks.

Yet friendship is based on reciprocity. Friends do not make exacting calculations on a week by week basis, but in the end they must maintain a balance, or resentment will creep in. In his astute book *Friendship: An Exposé*, Joseph Epstein writes, "A friend, a cliché definition has it, is someone who, when you are in crisis, you call at 4 a.m. I'd say that's true, but with the qualification that one is permitted only one such call."

Unless of course, the recipient of the call owes a favor that is at least as large. The intricacies can be extraordinarily wide-ranging and complex, spanning decades. Sometimes reciprocity descends into mechanicality: we invited them, they invited us, we invited them, and so on. Two couples may play this game for years after any pleasure in the relationship has evaporated.

At this point, a reader might be exasperated with my account, emphasizing as it does conditions, transactions, and reciprocation. My picture may seem cynical and one-sided. What, someone could ask, about the sheer joy of giving?

What indeed? There is real pleasure in giving, often even more than in receiving, but why should there be? Sociobiology, with its selfish genes and genetically motivated altruism, gives poor excuses for motivation. No one can believe these theories (at least not as a complete picture) without making a quasi-religious commitment to neo-Darwinism.

Selfish people view the joy of giving as self-delusion. They do not understand it, and if someone should give them something out of sheer goodness, they resent it, suspecting ulterior motives. There is something empty and defective in such people. Most intelligent adults recognize this but have little idea of why giving should be so rewarding in itself.

There is no answer in biology, in the social contract, even in religion. Moving into this question leads us to unconditional love. As I have suggested, it is rarer than most of us would like to admit, but it is real.

Unconditional love often has a random aspect: a stray act of kindness from a stranger to a stranger, with no expectation of return. (One of the most pungent things about New York City is that you can witness an act of extraordinary goodness and an act of gratuitous nastiness often within the same hour.) This love is unconditional because it passes between individuals who in all likelihood will never see each other again. No repayment is expected or usually possible.

The answer lies in the secret. It is the greatest of all secrets. Everyone knows it at some level, although for most people it is unconscious and unstated, felt and acted on but seldom articulated.

How often have we heard this: "We are all one"? Really? In what respect? In day-to-day life, we are most certainly not one. You want one thing; I want another. You are going there; I am coming here. This sentiment is often repeated, yet in ordinary terms, it is meaningless.

Only mysticism provides an answer. By *mysticism*, here I mean levels of inner insight and experience that go beyond the bounds of the psyche as commonly understood. Volumes upon volumes discuss mystical experience, and it has been illustrated by first-person accounts from all peoples in all ages.

Meditation provides a further key. In certain meditative states, you withdraw to an inner part of the self that views everything, ranging from ordinary physical sensations to your innermost thoughts and desires, from a third-person perspective. This experience is easy to generate. But what does it mean?

If you can observe all of these things—thoughts, dreams, desires, emotions, images, as well as impressions of the physical world—from a distance, it must follow that you are not where those things are. Therefore you are not those things, however much you may think you are. If you rest in a certain inner silence, you separate from all of these things and become aware of what has been called the *witness*. It has many other names too: Self, atman, the true "I." Strictly speaking, you will never be able to observe this Self, because *it is always what is observing*: it is you in your innermost reaches. You can never lose it. Nor does it ever die, although your body and even your personal psyche will eventually die.

For us most of the time, although the Self is always with us, it is usually hidden: we have buried it under layers of thoughts, desires, and wishes. As I have suggested in *Inner Christianity*, spiritual growth is a matter of awakening and identifying with this true "I," which is nothing more than our birthright, however completely we may have forgotten this truth.

Contact with the "true I" is one stage of awakening. Beyond it is a level that is still more remote and more difficult to describe, at which one realizes that this "I" is identical in all of us—all of humanity, of all animate life, possibly of inanimate life as well. This truth has been endlessly expressed, for example, in *A Course in Miracles*: "One brother is all brothers. Every mind contains all minds, for every mind is one. Such is the truth."

Some experience this truth directly. Here is one example, from Richard Bucke's classic *Cosmic Consciousness*, by a woman he identifies only as "C.M.C.":

I felt myself going, losing myself. Then I was terrified, but with a sweet terror. I was losing my consciousness, my identity, but was powerless to hold myself. Now came a period of rapture, so intense that the universe stood still, as if amazed at the unutterable majesty of the spectacle. Only one in all the universe! The All-loving, the Perfect One! The Perfect Wisdom, truth, love and purity. And with the rapture came the insight. In that same wonderful moment of what might be called supernal bliss, came illumination. I saw with intense inward vision the atoms or molecules, of which seemingly the universe is composed—I know not whether material or spiritual—rearranging themselves, as the cosmos (in its continuous, everlasting life) passes from *order to order*. What joy when I saw there was no break in the chain—not a link left out—everything in its place and time. Worlds, systems, all blended in one harmonious whole. Universal life, synonymous with universal love!

Here is the ultimate secret to the love game: the perception of the unity of all beings. A rare and lucky few, like C.M.C., are granted a vision of it consciously. I believe that anyone who has had such an experience will never be the same again—possibly will never again be able to hate.

Such visions are not given to everyone. They usually manifest, spontaneously and arbitrarily, to ordinary people (less often to the clergy, the present-day scribes and Pharisees). Other people grasp this truth intellectually or mechanically, parroting axioms like "We are all one" without any clear idea of what that means.

Another class of people understand this truth intuitively, even if they never come close to formulating it in words. They are the genuinely selfless people, because at some level of their minds, they understand that their interests are not separate from those of everyone else. They are the good people of the world—Jack Black's Johnson family.

No one can be completely cut off from this common life, because that would mean ceasing to exist. But its truth is not clear to the same degree in all minds. It is almost completely absent in sociopaths and psychopaths, who can only regard others as objects and instruments to be used. It is a bit more present in those who live according to religious precepts (because all religions teach this same truth in their own ways), but it may be heavily buried under a fear of the wrath of God.

There is an infinite number of gradations. They have nothing to do with class, race, religion, nationality, social status, or intellect. Simple, uneducated people sometimes show a clear understanding of this truth, whereas the learned are frequently blind to it. When I was at Oxford, a professor connected with my college was regarded as the leading moral philosopher in the English-speaking world. I talked to more than one of his graduate advisees who said he treated them detestably.

The love game has many tiers. At the most basic level is pure transaction. I go to the store to buy a gallon of milk; the clerk takes my money, and I go away with the milk. Few would call this love, but it is a satisfactory and often pleasant experience, even though that clerk and I may never see other again.

Above are the levels of professional relationship, in which people are often cordial and kind to one another, although business is always at the forefront.

Further up still are friendships, family relations, allegiances to social groups, religions, and nations. At the top are people like C.M.C. Not everyone can describe an experience this profound, but to the extent that we are kind, decent people, the recognition of ultimate unity is operating at the deepest layers of our minds.

Further discussion of these concepts will take us into the Master Game, which we shall explore in due course.

# 3

# Power

The dictate of a tyrant is an exercise of power. So is the cry of a newborn infant. Which has more force?

The tyrant's command has only as much strength as his henchmen can exercise. The infant's cry affects anyone who can hear it.

One classic definition of power is from Thomas Hobbes:

The power of *a man* ... is his present means, to obtain some future apparent good. ...

*Natural power*, is the eminence of the faculties of body, or mind: as extraordinary strength, form, prudence, arts, eloquence, liberality, nobility. *Instrumental* are those powers, which acquired by these, or by fortune, are means and instruments to acquire more.... For the nature of power, is in this point, like to fame, increasing as it proceeds.

For an infant, power consists in using the means available to it (such as crying) to obtain something (food, a diaper change) that it cannot provide for itself.

We all have to do the same thing every day of our lives. Asking a stranger on the street for directions is an exercise of power. You have no authority to enforce your request, but you are relying on the force of social expectations: normal, decent people are supposed to give directions to strangers. If a stranger asks you for directions, you are under the same pressure. In both cases, this is a perfectly standard request. If you ask a stranger for money, you may get an entirely different response, because social expectations are not on your side, or at any rate not as unambiguously. Here society leaves it purely to personal judgment whether someone gives you anything or not.

Again, it is all on a continuum. It costs nothing but a minute or two to give directions to a stranger and is usually repaid with nothing more than a thank-you.

On the other end is the story I heard from an influential public relations man. A client of his needed a favor (I assume of the political variety). The individual who could grant this favor was very hard to get access to. The PR man said he could make a call and it would go through, but that one call would cost the client $25,000. The call was made and the favor was granted. I imagine that the client considered it money well spent.

Early twentieth-century psychology had three giants: Sigmund Freud, who put the libido or the sex drive at the center of his system; C.G. Jung, who focused on the archetypes of the collective unconscious; and Alfred Adler, who based his psychology on the power dynamic.

Of these, the first two remain extraordinarily influential, but Adler has fallen into the background—probably unjustly. Sex, as Freud knew, is one major spring in the mechanism of the psyche, but that is principally true only in a circumscribed time of life—say, from puberty to menopause (male and female). Jung's archetypes certainly operate in all of us, but in practically everyone, they are unconscious.

Adler's view of power is in many ways the most compelling of the three views of psychology. Power is a matter of constant concern from cradle to deathbed. Even mere locomotion depends on power: if you don't have the 2,000 calories needed to function daily, eventually you won't be able to move. In his book *The 900 Days*, Harrison E. Salisbury somberly paints the city of Leningrad in the winter of 1941–42, during the worst of the Nazi blockade. At this time, rations were far below the necessary minimum; nor was there any heat.

Many of Salisbury's most vivid details have to do with the simple lack of power even to get up and move. People in those days did not lock their doors because if someone should come, they did not have the strength to answer. It was routine to see men and women dropping dead as they walked down the streets. People would leave dead family members in their homes for days, because even the living could barely get up, and the cold ensured that the bodies froze instead of rotting.

We can characterize all of the stages of human life in terms of power. One sometimes has the impression that infants cry, not because of hunger or a soiled diaper, but out of sheer frustration at their own helplessness.

When babies begin to crawl and walk with some confidence, power struggles shift to another stage. Parents soon learn that their children are stronger than they might have thought. (I was irked with the quality of Ikea furniture when I found that our one-year-old son had torn the front off the drawer of one of their bureaus.) Up to this point, the child has been able to do nothing for itself: its only recourse is its wails. Soon it discovers that it can do all sorts of things, but its parents object to them. (When our same son drank some lemon furniture oil, it was time to fire the baby sitter.) Of course the child does not understand why the parents find such things so obnoxious, so it protests, leading to the terrible twos.

With crises and lulls, this state of affairs prevails until adulthood. Parents want their children to eat food the children do not want to eat. They want them to stay close to home, although the children want to go off. The child wants to watch TV or play video games instead of submitting to the abuse of homework.

Puberty adds more conflicts. The adolescent wants to go still further afield, but this often makes parents anxious. Not without reason: crime, drugs, alcohol, and other misdoings are common among teenagers. Many families stumble when navigating through these obstacles, and many parents regard their children's teenage years as a savage initiation.

This conflict of wills begins to slack off when the child finishes formal education and goes off to earn an independent living. But usually the tension never goes away entirely. How many eighty-year-old men are still trying to subdue their fifty-year-old sons with their own expectations? Often only death, separation, or the extreme helplessness of one party or another brings this struggle to a complete end.

Because, as we shall see, humans are far from unified beings, power dynamics take place even within a single person. Every time another person is added, the complications multiply exponentially, so the picture becomes even more intricate when more than one child is involved. Siblings constantly vie over power. A child will exact a strict demand of justice—"That's not *fair!*"—but bristles when the same demand is placed on her.

The literature of the Western world is practically one long chronicle of such struggles within families—from the house of Atreus to the Tyrones of Eugene O'Neill's *Long Day's Journey into Night*. This play, which takes place during the course of a single day, portrays the tensions between two parents and their adult sons. The father, James Tyrone, is a retired actor who regrets that his career decisions brought him wealth but stifled him creatively. His wife, Mary, has recently returned from unsuccessful treatment for morphine addiction, which began when her stingy husband called in a cheap doctor who gave it to her during childbirth. The elder son, Jamie, is an actor like his father, but has trouble getting parts because of his drunkenness and unreliability. Edmund, the younger son, has artistic leanings but has been diagnosed with tuberculosis.

The entire action consists of power plays and manipulations. Mary refuses to believe Edmund's diagnosis, claiming that he is exaggerating; he retorts by saying how difficult it is "to have a dope fiend for a mother." Jamie confesses to Edmund that although he loves him more than anyone else, he has always wanted him to fail. Although the family members own up to their faults and feelings, there is no resolution. At the end of the play, Mary, high on morphine, comes down the stairs in her wedding gown, lamenting that falling in love with her husband caused her to lose her vocation as a nun.

Family dynamics aside, we generally think of power in much broader contexts. We have already seen Hobbes's definition as the "present means, to obtain some future apparent good." As Adler indicated, security is a major component:

> By security we do not consider only security from danger; we refer to that further coefficient of safety which guarantees the continued existence of the human organism under optimum circumstances, in very much the same way that we speak of the "coefficient of safety" in the operation of a well-planned machine. A child acquires this coefficient of safety by demanding a "plus" factor of safety greater than is necessary merely for the sat-

isfaction of his given instincts, greater than would
be necessary for a quiet development. This arise a
new movement in his soul life. This new movement
is, very plainly, a tendency toward domination and
superiority.

One could write a history of the human race in light of
these comments.

Survival is a matter of perpetuating the body. But
the body does not exist as an isolated object in space.
It lives in an environment, and it demands that this
environment enable it to live safely. Human beings
want to have safe homes as well as safe bodies. Power
is the means of creating this security. One element of
this power is ownership of territory. Your possession
of a house guarantees you the right to free and secure
access to the area that surrounds you. If you rent your
home, you have similar rights, although they are much
more limited.

Soon you realize that the safety of your property
requires much more than your mere right and ability
to protect it. You are concerned with the security of
your neighborhood, your town, your nation. The wider
the circle, the more nebulous and frightening the picture. You worry about your country's fate—often in
political terms, an "us" versus "them," Republican versus Democrat, blue state versus red state. People vex

themselves over the relative power of each; the "other" is always a knife to the country's jugular.

The number of sides? Two. The Russian philosopher P.D. Ouspensky discusses the "formatory center," which is his term for the mechanical aspect of the intellect:

> It is always possible to recognize "formatory thinking." For instance, the formatory center can only count up to two. It always divides everything in two: "bolshevism and fascism," "workers and bourgeois," "proletarians and capitalists," and so on. We owe most modern catchwords to formatory thinking, and not only catchwords but all modern popular theories. Perhaps it is possible to say that at all times all popular theories are formatory.

It is too simple to say that politicians make use of formatory thinking, because they are usually subject to it themselves.

Certainly political struggles in any state with some measure of freedom usually devolve into a clash between two parties: the rich, who are few but powerful, and everyone else. In the Athenian democracy of the fifth century BC, the higher class liked to style themselves *hoi kaloi k'agathoi* ("the beautiful and the good") as opposed to the *demos*, the people. The

Roman Republic, which was maturing in more or less the same era, distinguished between the patricians and the plebs, whose names have survived as English words.

In his commentary on Livy's history of Rome, Niccolò Macchiavelli wrote, "In every republic there are two opposed factions, that of the people and that of the rich, and . . . all the laws made in favor of liberty result from their discord." I leave it to the reader to decide how these forces manifest themselves in contemporary American politics.

To return to the level of the individual: security, the "present means, to achieve some apparent future good"—soon it becomes clear that some people go far past these objectives to seek out power for its own sake. Here the "apparent future good" is not some concrete object or possession, but power itself: the quest for power becomes a recursive game. In this it resembles money: the billionaire who bribes political leaders to cut his taxes does not need or even want more houses or cash or companies. The game is not about gaining more of something one already has in abundance. Money itself becomes the objective.

As I have already said, this kind of thirst is usually trying to compensate for some other, possibly more intense but less conscious, need that has never been met. In *Citizen Kane*, Jedidiah Leland says about his former friend, the millionaire publisher Charles Foster Kane, who unsuccessfully ran for office, "Love. That's why he did everything. That's why he went into politics. It seems we weren't enough, he wanted all the voters to love him too. Guess all he really wanted out of life was love. That's Charlie's story, how he lost it. You see, he just didn't have any to give. Well, he loved Charlie Kane of course, very dearly."

In his epilogue to *War and Peace*, Leo Tolstoy characterizes power as a kind of cone. At the base is the majority—in an army, the privates. They actually carry out the army's purposes—"the soldier directly stabs, cuts, burns, loots," but "always receives orders for those actions from higher-placed persons." Sergeants performs fewer of these actions and give some orders; officers give more orders and perform still direct actions. "The commander can never take a direct part in the action itself and only gives general instructions about the movement of the masses."

Tolstoy describes what he regards as the central fact of power:

For the carrying out of any joint action, people form themselves into such relations such that the more immediately people participate in the action, the less they can give orders and the greater their number; and the smaller the direct part people take in the action itself, the more they give the orders and the smaller their number, rising in this way from the lowest layers to the one last man, who takes the least direct part in the event and more than all aims his activity at giving orders.

Rising in one of these "cones" launches an individual into the power game proper. The first thing required is an arena—a setting in which power is sought and exercised. It may be a ladies' garden club, a school board, a department in a corporation, or the United States Senate. Even someone whose ambitions are large must usually start in an arena that is much smaller than the one that is the ultimate goal.

An enormous body of writing has sprung up about the nature and exercise of power. Fortunately for readers, this material is generally very redundant: each guide to power sounds more or less like the others. If you've read one, you've read them all.

One salient point is the stance—the attitude required to master this game. In his book *The Craft of Power*, R.G.H. Siu writes, "The primary rule is self-discipline—the severe self-discipline of dedication and destiny, of great tyrant and master robber. If you fail this first test, go no further. Melt into the acquiescent herd."

Self-discipline requires self-sacrifice. Everything else must be sacrificed to the primary goal. A power seeker cannot afford to be caught groping a secretary or photographed at a motel with a male whore. If he does, he puts himself out of the game.

Still more elementarily, Siu counsels, "Do not ruin it all by blurting out some accusations or losing your temper even once in public." To this we could add emotional breakdowns. When he was running for president in 1972, Senator Edmund Muskie was assailed by false accusations that he had made denigrating remarks about French Canadians and that his wife was a drunk. He gave his response in a snowstorm. Although he claimed that the tears that seemed to be running down his cheeks were melting snowflakes, observers believed that he was breaking down, ending his chances for the presidency.

The quest for power requires virtue, but of a unique sort, which does not always accord with either conventional morality or the highest ethical teachings of humankind. In *The Prince*, perhaps the most famous of all works on power, Machiavelli writes that the prince "needs to be so prudent that he escapes ill repute for such vices as may take his position away from him" but "does not even worry about incurring reproach for those vices without which he can hardly maintain his position, because when we carefully examine the whole matter, we find some qualities that look like virtues, yet—if the prince practices them—they will be his destruction, and other qualities that look like vices, yet—if he practices them—they will bring him safety and well-being."

Napoleon Hill, the well-known twentieth-century success guru, spelled out his principles for achievement in a number of works, such as *Think and Grow Rich*. He is sometimes derided as an example of the "dollars-want-me" positive thinking school, but thinking is only part of the picture. In fact the centerpiece of his method is the creation of a "definite major purpose," which you are supposed to set down in writing but share with no one else.

Hill has filled his books with examples of individuals who have achieved success this way, but I will recount one unusual story from my own experience.

Once in 1989, I was having dinner with some business associates in Cookeville or Crossville, Tennessee (I forget which; they are very close). It was at one of the strangest restaurants I have ever been to. It was huge, with many rooms, all of which were empty: ours was the only party there. It served only one dish: a creditable surf-and-turf combination. The proprietress had been a costumier in the Golden Age of Hollywood, and she had many costumes from that era on display, including one worn by Bette Davis in *The Private Lives of Elizabeth and Essex.*

The proprietress told a story about Ronald Reagan in his days as an actor. One day (I suppose around 1940) he showed up at the studio in a suit and tie. The other stars, who were sitting around in casual attire, sneered at him for being so elaborately dressed. He said, "You don't understand. Someday I'm going to be president of the United States."

Although I heard this story from the costumier's mouth, I have no way of verifying it. (I will say that she also read my palm that evening and made a prediction that was strikingly and unexpectedly accurate.) In any case, there are plenty of well-documented stories of similar aims set early and later achieved.

Although Hill says the "one definite purpose" is the key to success in any area, its importance is particularly evident in the quest for power. We admire Lincoln, yet I have read that he did not make one single step in his career that was not in some way targeted toward his political advancement. Those who seek political power rarely if ever go very far without this singleness of purpose.

The man whose exertion of will in the quest for power left the most powerful impression on the nineteenth century was Napoleon Bonaparte. He the scion of obscure Corsican nobility, yet he achieved so many military successes that in 1799, when he was thirty years old (and a mere six years after the French had beheaded their king), he was named First Consul—effectively supreme dictator. Five years later, he was crowned as emperor of France.

The great tyrants of the twentieth century achieved successes that were even more astonishing, although these were less the result of extraordinary genius and ability than of supremacy in megalomania, lies, and cruelty.

In short, power seems to be a function of individual will. This explains why so few people achieve power in any sphere. The typical human is a fragmented creature, motivated by vague wishes that are usually overruled by a pack of fears. The extent to which this is the case determines how far the individual will advance. Some will sacrifice their families in order to climb some staircase of success, only to discover that winning at one game means losing at another. Some swim back and forth, unsure and therefore unachieving. Still others achieve a contented balance between all their needs and settle into comfortable if unremarkable lives.

Unless your aim is to be lord of a desert island, the quest for power necessarily involves other people. You may think in terms of friends and enemies, but in the realms of power, this is an error. Here there are no friends or enemies, merely allies and opponents, and any party can switch almost immediately from one to the other. Forgetting this fact is one of the commonest mistakes in history.

To pick one example, at a late stage the Roman Republic was dominated by a triumvirate of three men: Julius Caesar, Gnaeus Pompey, and Marcus Licinius Crassus. This alliance was cemented by family relations: Pompey married Caesar's daughter. After she died and Crassus was killed fighting the Parthians, the two survivors fell out, precipitating the outbreak of the Roman Civil War in 49 BC. Three years later, Pompey was defeated and killed, leaving Caesar in triumph until he was assassinated in the Senate building in 44 BC. Caesar fell dead at the foot of Pompey's statue.

The reverse happens just as often. Hitler's invasion of the Soviet Union in 1941 transformed Stalin overnight from an opponent of the Western powers to an ally.

In a hierarchy, power relations divide all concerned into three categories: superiors, peers, and subordinates. Any of these can switch from ally to opponent and back again. In most situations, you will find it hard to advance unless your boss is on your side. If your boss turns into an opponent, it is possible to go over his head, but that is a declaration of war.

Since the balance of power is not on your side, you will (intentionally or not) usually end up losing.

One common but stupid tactic is to curry favor with superiors, regard peers as rivals, and view subordinates as insignificant. You certainly want the approval and support of your bosses, but it should be for your achievements rather than obsequiousness. Machiavelli advises the prince on how to avoid flatterers:

> There is no other way for securing yourself against flatteries except that men understand that they do not offend you by telling the truth; but when everybody can tell you the truth, you fail to get respect. Hence a prudent prince uses a third method, choosing for his government wise men and to them alone giving free power to tell him the truth, but on such things only as he asks about, and on nothing else. But he asks them about everything and listens to their opinions; and he decides for himself, at his own pleasure, on the basis of their advice; and with each of them he so bears himself that every adviser realizes that the more freely he speaks, the better he is received.

If your boss is a "prudent prince," it is best to follow Machiavelli's advice and speak frankly as a subordinate, but only on questions asked.

Even so, many leaders are susceptible to bowing and scraping. In these cases, it is best to focus on doing one's job with excellence and nothing else, because such superiors will never be reliable allies. Often their vanities cover so many weaknesses that you may soon find yourself dealing with a different boss anyway.

Peers—people at your level of the hierarchy—have no power over you, and you have no power over them. Because hierarchies are pyramidal, each level has fewer places the farther up you go, so people often regard peers as rivals. A decent organization might encourage competition between peers in excelling at their tasks but would refrain from pitting them against one another personally. Many companies violate this rule, promoting rivalry and mutual sabotage, and remain successful. But in these situations, you have to ask yourself whether you even want to survive in such an environment.

The modern business organization is structured so that workers are regarded as replaceable parts. Of course, this is bad business practice, if only because it costs a great deal of money and time to replace any employee who quits. Furthermore, each new worker, no matter how experienced, is a beginner in the company and a stranger to its ways, so the company has to start over again with each and every one.

We could ask whether the Great Resignation—the desertion of their jobs by millions of Americans in 2021–22—is inspiring managers to change this view. Some have said so. But executives often spout the rhetoric of care and compassion while remaining utterly unconcerned with anything of the kind.

If you have subordinates, you have to free yourself of this line of thinking, no matter how ingrained it may be in the organizational mentality. The most obvious reason is that your success depends on theirs. You cannot deliver the results required of you without their help, and your behavior toward them will in large part determine whether they stay with the company. "You don't quit your job; you quit your boss," it is said.

Whether the company's leaders have any human feeling or not, they understand that there is a such a thing as high turnover and that it is bad. Sometimes a good manager has to serve as a buffer, protecting his department from stupid orders from his superiors. Furthermore, it is never wise to underestimate the extent to which your subordinates can sabotage you.

Such are the rules in hierarchies, but other power structures exist as well. The United States government is based on democracy, which means the consent and support of the governed. If you are an elected official, you have some (sometimes complete) autonomy from hierarchical control, but here your power lies with your constituents. Siu counsels:

> In order that your constituency will stand firm in support of you, three requirements must be met. First, that they feel you are one of them; at the very least, your heart is with them. Second, that they remain satisfied with your services to them. Third, that no more than a scattered few among them harbor any hatred toward you.

I suspect that if you examine the career of any long-standing legislative politician, you will find that these rules apply.

Up to now, we have been discussing power dynamics in more or less normal circumstances. Unfortunately, this in no way encompasses the complete range of the subject. A large amount of the population (in this country or any other) is made up of people with personality disorders. Many of them fixate on using power in dysfunctional ways. In their book *Toxic Coworkers*, psychologists Alan A. Cavaiola and Neil J. Lavender identify the array of mental disorders in the workplace. One hypothetical case:

If . . . Mr. Allen, a narcissistic middle manager for a large medical laboratory, verbally abuses his staff, ignores cost-saving ideas, or continuously make administrative decisions that only benefit him, then he will incur enormous hidden costs. What are some of these costs? Higher rates of absenteeism; undermining loyal employees' commitment to the organization; reduction in employee self-esteem, creating a sense of malaise, high turnover and retraining costs; higher levels of stress accompanied by increases in stress-related accidents; resistance to new managerial directives; counsel fee; litigation including high settlement fee and jury awards; just to name a few. And the number of hours spent discussing the problems will increase until Mr. Allen is eventually identified as the problem. And, in the case of a well-paid, high-profile administrator, it could often take years before workers are willing to come forward to address the administrator's problems.

Still worse, dysfunctional individuals are often adept at working around the rules or nominally complying with them. I doubt that there are many people in the workforce who have not had to deal with someone of this kind. "Our own study of personality factors and stress in the workplace showed that over 80 percent of our sample worked with at least one individual whose behavior was a significant source of stress for them," write Cavaiola and Lavender.

Some employees deal with both violent threats and institutional apathy. Here is one case, from real life: "I knew I had to leave this job when an employee threatened me with a knife and called me the 'N-word.' My manager told me I had to understand where he was coming from."

From here we proceed to intentional abuses of power, many of which involve crime. It was long believed that crime was the result of poverty, although it may be more accurate to say that poverty is a result of crime. Crime is so intricately tied to present society that we tend to regard it as normal or at any rate unavoidable. It operates on a scale much larger than is usually imagined. The esoteric philosopher Rodney Collin writes:

Many things which society itself supports and justifies as "patriotism," "loyalty," "freedom," "duty," "responsibility" and so on, may contain a strong criminal tendency. To what other process, for example, can belong propaganda, which—ingeniously using the skill of the artist, the experience of the psychology, and the technique of the scientist— endeavours to put to sleep or destroy natural living judgment and replace it with a single standardised attitude, temporarily expedient from the point of view of a single policy, a single government or a single advertiser?

Anyone who believes that Collin is exaggerating should look at the uses to which the concept of freedom has been put in the United States recently. Any and every sort of abuse has been justified on the grounds that someone—an individual, a company, an interest group—is entitled to "freedom." At this point, whenever "freedom" is invoked in public discourse, one ought to ask which lies it is intended to conceal or which crimes it is meant to justify.

Political liberty and civil rights exist in America today largely because no one set of lies has been able to establish itself completely at the expense of the others.

Tyranny, of course, is the ultimate abuse of power, and it is not easy to explain why it has been able to establish itself so often and been so difficult to tear down. The Polish theorist Andrew M. Lobaczewski wrote a book on the subject called *Political Ponerology*. *Ponerology* is derived from the Greek *poneros*, "wicked," and, as the subtitle of his book has it, is "a science on the nature of evil as adjusted for political purposes."

Lobaczewski contends that those responsible for "pathocracies"—states ruled by psychopaths—are suffering from acute mental dysfunctions.

Every society contains a certain percentage of people carrying psychological deviations caused by various inherited or acquired factors, which produce anomalies in thought, perception, and character. Many such people attempt to impart meaning to their deviant lives by means of social hyperactivity. They create their own ideologies and myths of overcompensation and have the tendency to egotistically insinuate to others that their own deviant perceptions and the resulting goals and ideas are superior.

Psychopaths, he continues, "very early learn how their personalities can have traumatizing effects on the personalities of normal people, and how to take advantage of this root of terror for purposes of reaching their goals."

Once these individuals find some organization that suits their purposes,

they begin infiltrating the rank and file of such a movement; pretending to be sincere adherents poses no difficulty for the psychopath, since it is second nature for them to play a role and hide behind the mask of normal people.... They initially perform subordinate functions in such a movement and execute the leaders' orders, especially whenever something needs to be done which inspires revulsion in others.... Thus they climb up the organizational ladder, gain influence, and almost involuntarily bend the contents of the entire group to their own way of experiencing reality and to the goals derived from their deviant nature.

If such a group gains control of a government through revolution, Lobaczewski continues, the government is transformed into a "macrosocial pathological phenomenon. Within this system the common man is blamed for *not* having been born a psychopath, and is considered is good for nothing but hard work, fighting and dying to protect a system of government he can neither sufficiently comprehend nor ever consider to be his own."

It is grim to consider how hundreds of millions of people have lived their entire lives under such systems.

People commonly think that psychopaths have the advantage over normal, decent people, because, unlike the latter, they are happy to pursue any and all means to achieve their ends. This is not entirely true. Psychopaths labor under one tremendous disability:

they are crazy. Therefore they view reality in distorted and bizarre ways, which hinders them from governing in a way that actually enables the society to function. The psychopaths in power, then, are in a sense at the mercy of normal people, who can make things work and who moreover greatly outnumber them.

Furthermore, as Lobaczewski points out, normal people soon figure out ways of evading the pathocrats' attempts at total control: they manage to communicate in oblique ways that get around the system. All of this makes the pathocratic system extremely unstable, and it will ultimately fall, either because it cannot keep the machinery of society functioning (as appears to be happening in present-day Venezuela), it overextends itself to the point of self-destruction (as in Nazi Germany), or the system's failures become so evident that the entire country gives up on it (as in the Soviet Union).

All these considerations show that power comes in many disparate forms. The Wiccan activist Starhawk summarizes the main types in her book *Truth or Dare*.

The first is "power-over." This kind of power depends totally on one's particular role in society or in an organization. Say a man is vice president of operations for a major corporation. He holds enormous power over the workings and personnel of an extremely large and complex organization. One day he is told his services are no longer required. Immediately his power vanishes. Nobody in the company has to obey him; in fact they are usually told not to. In one day, he is no longer even welcome in his own office.

This kind of power is the most evanescent. Sane people in these positions understand this fact and retain some humility, realizing that they hold authority only in circumscribed conditions, which could change very fast and very soon. Abnormal people in these positions forget the difference between themselves and their titles, perpetrating excesses and abuses which usually lead to their downfall.

The second form of power, according to Starhawk, is "power-with, or influence: the power of a strong individual in a group of equals, the power not to command, but to suggest and be listened to, to begin something and see it happen. The source of power-with is the willingness of others to listen to our ideas."

Successful activists possess power-with. They usually hold no official positions of any great authority: their influence lies in their charisma and the truth of what they say. Figures like Gandhi and Martin Luther King Jr. exemplify power-with.

Finally there is "power-from-within":

Power-from-within is . . . akin to something deeper. It arises from our sense of connection, our bonding

with other human beings, and with the environment. . . .

Power-from-within sustains our lives. We can
feel that power in acts of creation and connection,
in planting, building, writing, cleaning, healing,
soothing, playing, singing, making love. We can feel
it in acting together with others.

I do not believe that power-with can be generated
except through power-from-within.

William Styron's novel *The Confessions of Nat Turner*
tells of the great slave revolt in 1831 Virginia that killed
fifty-five whites. A key moment comes when Nat
Turner, the leader of the revolt, realizes his power over
another slave, named Willis. "Then for the first time
like a yellow burst of sunlight which steals out from
behind a cloud and floods the day, there swept over me
the mysterious sense of my own hidden yet implacable
and onrushing power." Without this power, Nat never
could have raised the insurrection.

Power-from-within—power in the ultimate sense—
is connection with the life force, universally known
under countless names, such as chi or prana. It cannot be overcome by any other force in the world: only
an equal or greater measure of the same power can
obstruct it. It is present in all of us: it is what makes the
difference between a living person and a corpse. But it

is not available to all equally. Many people have it only in attenuated form as a result of physical weakness, injury, trauma, or psychological blocks.

Some naturally have this power in abundance; others acquire it through overcoming the oppositions of life; still others, through certain spiritual and mystical practices.

People who possess large measures of this power do not always use it intelligently or humanely, as the history of Nat Turner suggests. To both cultivate this power and have the wisdom to use it is the prerogative of those who play the Master Game.

# 4

# Pleasure

*There never has been, there is not, and there never will*
*be anything that will appear to us superior to what we*
*desire. It is the essence of all action. There lie the ideas*
*of duty and wealth. As cream is the essence of milk,*
*pleasure is the essence of duty, the source of wealth.*

—THE MAHABHARATA

Survival, love, power—these are all primal games. Yet pleasure comes before all of these. Practically everything we do is to promote pleasure or avoid pain, now or in the future. We would not do anything without this motive. You would not even know whether you were succeeding in the games of love, survival, or power without a sense of pleasure.

Epicurus, the philosopher of pleasure par excellence, said that the beginning and root of every good is the pleasure of the stomach. Some have criticized him for being too base-minded, but he was right: what would you be able to enjoy if you were hungry?

Epicurus's philosophy inspired Lucretius' *De rerum natura* ("The Nature of Things"). Written in the first century BC, it has been called the greatest poem in the Latin language. At the beginning, Lucretius, addressing Venus, writes:

*You alone guide all the things of nature;*
*without you nothing arises on the shores of light,*
*nor is anything lovely or anything glad.*

Here the poet is not so much addressing the Venus of Greco-Roman religion as harking back to the primordial religion of humanity. At that time there were not gods of love, of the sea, or thunder: rather, those entities were themselves the gods—natural forces that could also interact personally with humans. The Hindu Rig Veda, for example, has a hymn to a wind god named Vata, but Vata is not the god of the wind: Vata *is* the wind. In the same way, Venus here is not the goddess of pleasure: she is pleasure itself.

Another early Greek philosopher, Empedocles, said that love and strife were the forces that governed the universe: "In strife are all things different and separate, but in love they come together and long for one another, and from these arise all that was, all that is, and all that shall be."

This may sound quaint, but we only have to translate these verses more idiomatically to bring them into focus: "In *repulsion* are all things different and separate, but in *attraction* they come together." With this twist, Empedocles' theory sounds startlingly modern and scientific.

We can take this concept further. In my book *The Dice Game of Shiva*, I suggested that consciousness, which I defined as the distinction of self from other, was the ground of the universe. In the fourteen years since the book's publication, I have seen many items in the scientific press that are driving toward this same conclusion, often in much the same terms.

Inanimate particles do not have a self-aware, introspective consciousness, but they distinguish between *self* and *other*. Thomas Edison made this point in an interview: "I do not believe . . . that matter is inert, acted upon by an outside force. To me it seems that every atom is possessed by a certain amount of primitive intelligence. Look at the thousands of ways in which atoms of hydrogen combine with those of other elements, forming the most diverse substances. Do you mean to say that they do this without intelligence?"

Each submolecular particle is attracted to certain other particles and repulsed by others. Is it too much to say that these particles take *pleasure* in those they find attractive?

Maybe atoms and molecules feel some rudimentary pleasure; we humans certainly do. A later philosopher, Jeremy Bentham in nineteenth-century England, explains:

> Nature has placed mankind under the governance of two sovereign masters, *pain* and *pleasure*. It is for them alone to point out what we ought to do, as well as to determine what we shall do. On the one hand the standard of right and wrong, on the other the chain of causes and effects, are fastened to their throne. They govern us in all we do, in all we say, in all we think: every effort we can make to throw off our subjection, will serve but to demonstrate and confirm it.

After this brisk stride through the philosophy of pleasure, we can look how Americans view it. Alexis de Tocqueville's remark in his classic *Democracy in America* is telling: "The cares of political life engross a most prominent place in the occupation of a citizen in the United States: and almost the only pleasure of which an American has any idea, is to take a part in the Government, and to discuss the part he has taken."

Writing in the 1830s, de Tocqueville is no doubt reflecting the naive patriotism of the early republic; today we would have to add the delights of making money. Indeed making money appears to be the only source of pleasure that the typical American can indulge in without feeling some measure of guilt. In many ways we are a nation of salesmen.

In a recent column in *The Atlantic*, Arthur C. Brooks contrasts pleasure with enjoyment:

> *Enjoyment* and *pleasure* are terms often used interchangeably, but they are not the same thing. Pleasure happens to you; enjoyment is something that you create through your own effort. Pleasure is the lightheadedness you get from a bit of grain alcohol; enjoyment is the satisfaction of a good wine, properly understood. Pleasure is addictive and animal; enjoyment is elective and human.

All true, to be sure. Yet twenty years ago, I had lunch at the home of a rich man in New York. White wine was served.

"Wow!" I said when I tasted it. "What *is* that wine?"

"Oh," replied, "just a little Montrachet."

The wine was superb, but I wonder if I would have enjoyed it as much if I had Montrachet at every lunchtime.

You could reverse Brooks' definitions: you could just as easily say that pleasure is earned and enjoyment unearned. Nevertheless, his view is profoundly American. We as a nation value nothing more than work; no enjoyment is morally legitimate without it. Even the most ostentatiously lazy of the rich must pretend they are doing something of value—sponsoring some cause, creating a fashion line that (we are told) is all about making a better world. It is unsurprising for an American to say that mere pleasure—ephemeral and completely unearned—is hardly worth bothering about.

A hundred years ago, Americans were ridiculed for their puritanical and hypocritical attitude toward sex—an attitude that appears to have largely vanished. It is no longer de rigueur to despise the enjoyment afforded by the genitals, but Americans do not appear to enjoy the sex act any more for all that. An advice column ran this query from a reader:

> I never enjoyed oral sex with my ex-husband, who was my only romantic partner in 40 years. Since my divorce, I have had sex with a couple of men, both of whom wanted to perform oral sex on me. This is something I have never felt comfortable with. Is it me? I feel I can never be clean enough, or that I may smell. Friends tell me it is awesome, and I do want

the best sex with my new partners, but I worry that there is something wrong with me.

This woman's grandmother would probably have bristled at the thought of cunnilingus; her mother might have felt guilty for enjoying it; she feels guilty for *not* enjoying it. Possibly she would have been reassured by this observation from G. Legman's 1969 work *Oragenitalism*: "Far from dissuading men from cunnilinctus—although, of course, it does dissuade many—this combined olfactory and gustatory experience may be a large or even the largest part of the man's desire to engage in cunnilinctus."

Cunnilingus is, as it were, a matter of taste: some women enjoy it, some do not. In any event, American guilt about sex has been displaced from remorse over having it to remorse over not doing it right.

On the male side, there was the man who wrote to a sex advice columnist, "I feel like I'm using my wife, or I feel selfish and self-conscious, especially when coming in her mouth (which I love to do, but feel very selfish!)."

I could find many other examples: performance anxiety in men; female worries about the difficulties of reaching orgasm; feeling desires for the wrong sex, whichever one that may be. I once knew a gay man who was disturbed because he was having heterosexual dreams. The variations are as endless as those of the act itself.

An example from the other end of the spectrum—those who take extreme pleasure in sex—is the "goonettes," women who "gather on sites like Reddit and devote themselves to porn and sometimes IRL [in real life] sexual escapades," according to an article on the Input website. "These women view pornography addiction as a fetish they engage in—not an ailment that besets them—and they pride themselves on their lengthy masturbation sessions, during which they consume as much adult content as possible—the more graphic, the better." (Male practitioners are called "gooners.") A Reddit site, r/GoonetteHub, has 31,000 members.

One fascinating feature of gooning is "edging."

"Goonettes will edge themselves on the brink of orgasm through intense masturbation to pornography, sometimes for hours or even days, until they transcend arousal into a gooning state," explains Duffy, who is 34 and from Ireland. "In this state, the pleasure experienced is beyond that of orgasm. Your body ends up shaking violently, you struggle to talk, and the only thing that matters is consuming more porn and maintaining your edge."

These women seem to have discovered an age-old secret on their own: delayed orgasm leads to heightened full-body pleasure. This appears to be a central goal of Tantric sex, at least as it is taught in the US.

Gooning is centered on finding pornography in itself—quite apart from any people it may represent—as the turn-on. Some may consider this abnormal, although for one who has difficulty with relationships, it may be less problematic than dealing with a real man or woman.

In any event, gooning illustrates one truth: it is possible to take any of these games (in this case, pleasure) and make it *the* game. "I ended up skipping work again to goon again today," writes one woman on the Reddit goonette site.

Is pleasure a matter of quantity, quality, or both? Does a man who wolfs down a fast-food meal enjoy it more or less than a gourmet at a five-star restaurant? There is no objective way of measuring quantities here. Especially with food, appetite accounts for a large degree of enjoyment. Hunger is the best of all spices, says one proverb.

All the same, there seems to be a hierarchy of pleasures. Refined connoisseurship is widely taken to be better than coarser satisfactions. According to such a view, there is more pleasure to be had in a first-rate Burgundy than in a can of lite beer.

What lies behind this attitude? Although some people have refined tastes instinctively, usually some education of taste is necessary. This in turn requires some amount of wealth: you will not learn to appreciate the finest wines if you can't afford them. It also requires leisure. To become an art connoisseur, you have to spend time in museums and galleries, and, often, to take some art history courses to appreciate what you are seeing.

I have educated tastes in some areas but not in others. I have read widely in world literature, so I don't enjoy trashy best sellers. Years ago, when I was writing book reviews for the *San Francisco Chronicle*, I went to its offices. Among the books that had come in was the latest Danielle Steel novel. I didn't know anything about Danielle Steel except that she was very popular, so I asked to review it. The editor agreed, looking at me with some misgiving. I did not get far, and returned the book unread and unreviewed.

On the other hand, my tastes in music are not particularly cultivated. If someone tells me that there is much more going on in one of Beethoven's late quartets than in the current pop hit, I believe him, but it is not a difference that I'm equipped to appreciate. I tend to listen to classical music only late in the evening as a means of relaxation. During the day, like many Americans, I listen to pop and rock songs because they have the effect (fully intended, I'm sure) of a mildly exhilarating stimulant—like a lightly caffeinated beverage that helps get you through your day.

Since sophisticated tastes are to some degree learned, and this learning takes time and money, refined pleasures are associated with high status. Over a century ago, Thorstein Veblen's *Theory of the Leisure Class* showed the intricate link between leisure and status.

It is prestigious to take pleasure in certain things rather than others. Of all the wines, the one most associated with prestige is champagne, largely because of its cost (the traditional *méthode champenoise* used to make it is very labor-intensive), although to my mind, it is the most overrated beverage in the world. I have had some wines whose quality has stunned me—chiefly red Bordeaux (not to mention Montrachet)—but none of them have been champagnes. An anonymous friend sent a bottle of Dom Pérignon to my wife and me as a wedding present. It was very enjoyable, but not in proportion to its cost. I did not think it was ten or twelve times better than a ten-dollar bottle of Spanish cava. (Naive of me to assume it should. I once asked a wine writer friend about the relation of quality to price in wine, and he replied, "None.")

Of the fine champagnes, I do like Roederer Brut for its bright, lemony quality but have not been impressed with many of the others. A Russian friend once brought over a bottle of her country's champagne, and I did like its flowery taste, although it probably would not pass the rigid requirements for dryness that present taste enforces upon this wine in the West.

I am not entirely alone in my opinion of champagne. In his delightful book *In Praise of Wine*, Alec Waugh writes:

No wine has been more ill-used. No wine has suffered more at the hands of malefactors. I am tempted indeed to parody the opening lines of *A Tale of Two Cities*: it is the best of wines, it is the worst of wines. It is an absurdly expensive wine.... It is associated with some of our most pleasant experiences and some of the most disagreeable—particularly in our youth, when we are short of money.... How often have we not all of us been forced to buy it when we could ill afford it in nightclubs where it was *obligatoire* and by venial ladies in league with the headwaiter—and how bad such wine invariably was. How often have we not been embarrassed and exasperated by the obnoxious vulgarians who will say, "Let us have wine tonight," as though claret and burgundy were not wines. How often have we not been stinted because a host has considered the presence of champagne a sufficient token of hospitality and has let one bottle do the work of two. I will not say, "Of no other wine have I such unpleasant memories;" that would be unfair to wine. I will omit the "such."

Waugh is looking back to his youth in 1920s Britain, but with the change of a few details, the picture remains accurate.

We then have to ask the unanswerable question: how many people like champagne because they are *supposed* to like champagne? We could say the same of many other refinements. Despite the virtuosity and beauty in ballet and opera, how many people like these arts because they are supposed to?

Writer Ling Ma describes a similar sentiment in a story about a young Chinese girl who has just come to America and tastes ice cream for the first time. "Breyer's French Vanilla. It's denser and sweeter than I expected, eggy in flavor, fuzzy with freezer burn. To my surprise, I don't like it at all and feel nauseated by its smell. But I have to like it, because I saw ice cream on TV back home, where all my friends and I fantasized how wonderful it must taste."

Indeed pleasure is a standardized commodity—issued in off-the-rack form, with some variations for social class. In an early issue of the *National Lampoon*, humorist Roger Price skewers the "Roob"—not the old-time hayseed rube, who "in his own environment . . . possessed many virtues: courage, loyalty, honesty and the basic virtue from which all others must stem—pride." But "once the rube . . . went to the City, he became a misplaced person and began to act badly again. He found himself in an anonymous urban society which neither threatened nor challenged him and which made no demands on him except as a Consumer. He became a Roob, with a capital R."

Over fifty years later, the type remains familiar:

You must understand the awesome importance to Roobs of the Vacation or the Weekend Trip. An exhausting and dangerous drive on a crowded thruway to an equally crowded and over-priced resort is their claim to membership in the Leisure Class. They go in search of the Pepsi People, the Ale Men, the Swingers; and they live in deadly fear that they may take the wrong road, read the wrong travels and not see the turnoff to Marlboro country. They are afraid they will *miss something*.

The Roob believes with all his heart that somewhere along Route 12A all the Fun People are having a Fun Time under the benevolent eye of a recreational counselor. No right-minded Fun Person would ever isolate himself or seek his own diversions, for a Roob's identity is based on attendance at mass functions that require standing in line, such as a company barbecue or the opening of a snake farm.

When Price was writing in 1970, the great Roob Valhalla, Disney World, was still under construction. But his article could have been used as a bible for marketing to the theme park's audience, who must adore "mass functions that require standing in line," the activity that occupies most of the time of any visitor.

My father-in-law was gracious enough to take our family to Disney World a few years ago. It was not a trip that I would have paid for on my own. Sweltering heat, shoulder-to-shoulder crowds, and staggeringly priced refreshments occupy much of my memory of it, even though it was October, a putatively cooler time of year and an off season because all the kids were supposed to be in school.

I remember a couple of amusing moments. When waiting in the security line, I was standing behind a man who, for reasons he did not appear to understand, was prohibited from bringing in his Bowie knife. It was a beautiful knife—brightly burnished steel, a handsomely crafted bone handle, perhaps a foot long. He did not relish having to hand it over to security, but he said his car was parked too far away for him to go back. So he handed it over, grumbling but resigned to never seeing it again.

I was taken with the knife as an object of craft, and it occurred to me to take him aside, offer him a few dollars for it, and hide it in the bushes to take back to the motel later. But I didn't. It was one of those small but nagging regrets that one sometimes has in life.

On another occasion, my family and I were standing in yet another line for yet another ride. Over the loudspeaker came the routine safety announcements in English and Spanish. Our sons were then enrolled in a bilingual program in their primary school, with many subjects taught in Spanish. When the announcement was over, I looked down to my elder son, Robert, and asked, "How much of that announcement did you understand?"

He looked up at me, beaming proudly, and said, "None." He did not take to bilingual education.

I wanted to take my children to Disney World, if only because, like many middle-class Americans, I had a half-submerged fear that if we did not give them this experience at least once, social workers would whisk them away from us as unsatisfactory parents. But I know several adults who enjoy going to Disney World for its own sake, probably for reasons sketched out by Roger Price. As a Broadway producer, the father of a school friend, once quipped to me, "One man's Mede is another man's Persian."

In the end, pleasure comes down to taste, some of it natural, some acquired through social conditioning. Even this age of idolizing personal idiosyncrasies tends to overlook the centrality of taste. Sexual preferences—gay, straight, lesbian, trans—are usually framed in terms of identities. But this is unwise. It forces people into conceptual boxes that do not take their own tastes for variation into account (as with the gay man who was disturbed by heterosexual dreams). This focus on identity leads to an identity politics that is often distorted or insane.

As Michel Foucault showed, homosexuality as a category and identity is a conceptual construction assembled over the past two centuries, although people indulged in homosexual acts before that—indeed for as long as history records. Before that, it was a practice, though a sinful one: sodomy as forbidden by the Bible. Evangelical attempts at "curing" homosexuals is a hybrid of these two ways of thought: an attempt to change an identity because it is sinful.

Seeing the issue as a matter of taste strikes me as far more civilized. I am reminded of a passage in André Malraux's novel *Man's Fate*, set in the China of the 1930s, in which two revolutionaries are deciding on their tactics against Nationalist leader Chiang Kai-shek. "It's only a question of deciding whether it's better to attack him as a pederast or accuse him of being bought," says one.

"It being perfectly understood that he is neither," replies the other. "Moreover, I don't like to have one of my collaborators believe me capable of attacking a man for a sexual deviation which he might really have. Do you take me for a moralist?"

It is as if it were legitimate to attack Chiang for pederasty as long as he is not a pederast, but not if he actually has a taste for pederasty.

No doubt certain sexual acts—particularly those involving coercion or children—will always and rightly be condemned. But in the long run, as mainstream culture gradually legitimizes alternative sexual preferences, it may put less and less emphasis on identity and acknowledge sexual tastes as what they are: tastes, which may vary over the years or even over a week. After all, people who like Chinese or Indian food generally do not want it every evening.

Even so, most people believe that a long-term, committed relationship with a single partner is the ideal for happiness. In such cases a choice of a partner means a choice of sexual identity perforce. Perhaps with some curious complications. Say one member of a lesbian couple decides to become a trans male. Does that make the other partner now a heterosexual?

Should we live for pleasure? The medieval fantasyland known as Cockaigne was a paradise of pleasures. In this mythical country, cherries grew on the ground so that you did not have to reach up to pick them, and they had sugar at their centers instead of hard pits. Fully cooked pigs would run up to you saying, "Eat me," and the houses were made of sausages and meats, nailed together with cinnamon and cloves. Sexual freedom reigned: the more promiscuous a woman was, the more she was held in esteem.

Moral license went beyond sensory indulgence. According to one account,

> Whosoever is found to be the biggest good-for-nothing, the most untrustworthy, rudest, most dull-witted, and moreover the laziest, most debauched vagabond and champion rogue—such a person is proclaimed king. . . .
>
> If here in this country there are any prodigal children who intend to display such manners as those written of above—by abandoning all pretense to honor, virtue, honesty, and civility, not to mention wisdom and knowledge—then those uncouth louts should go to that land, where, upon their

arrival, they will undoubtedly be respected and esteemed.

The fable of Cockaigne teaches that it is a fault of character to live purely for pleasures, whether they involve gorging on food, video games, or day-long masturbation sessions with porn.

One great contemporary philosopher of pleasure was the late Hugh M. Hefner, publisher of *Playboy* and founder of a titillating nightclub empire. But even he acknowledges the need for something beyond:

> We believe that life can be a greater pleasure if it is lived with some style and grace and comfort and beauty, but we do not believe that these are the all of it. It is possible to become so caught up in the trappings—both the form and the accoutrements of living—that the real satisfactions become lost. Each man—and woman—should try to know himself, as well as the world around him, and take real pride in that knowledge.

This passage is taken from *The Playboy Philosophy*, a series of essays published by Hefner in his magazine in the early 1960s.

Beyond mere hedonism lies connoisseurship, which turns pleasures into refinements. The enophile who can with a mere sip say which vineyard a particular Burgundy comes from down to the square meter, and the art collector who can look at a putative Old Master and tell within a second whether it is authentic, have gone far beyond the bounds of mere hedonism. But yet again, the games overlap, and at this point the pleasure game merges with the game of creativity.

All this said, it has long been known that pleasure and desire point toward something beyond themselves—beyond even the objects toward which they are directed. The French philosopher Alain Daniélou observes:

The extreme sensation of pleasure is considered to be the image, the reflection of the infinite pleasure that the individual experiences when united with universal or divine Being.

The discovery of divine reality is for many beings, perhaps all, linked to that of human love. In the first sexual act of the adolescent, all of the suffering of life seems to dissipate, disappearing in the wonder of happiness. In this first instant, he often discovers a direct notion of the divine: "There is a God, because so much joy is possible." And this thought remains fixed forever. It is the source of all religion.

Daniélou goes on to say that the intense joy of sexual fulfillment "resembles the state of pleasure described by the mystics of all religions when they finally achieve contact with the divine lover."

Some mystics would go further, arguing that the pleasures of physical love are misdirected spiritual impulses—a longing for the divine displaced onto human objects. We need not agree with them fully to see some merit in their claim.

# 5

# Creativity

The rise and fall of civilizations have occupied the greatest minds of the West. That they have never come up with an adequate explanation shows the difficulty of the problem.

We have no way of understanding why the Mayans built an enormous and complex civilization in Central America only to have it suddenly collapse, leaving its great pyramids to be covered by jungle and its memory forgotten even by its creators' descendants.

The fall of the Roman Empire haunts the civilization that inherited its legacy. The West remains constantly in fear that it may happen again: the *Untergang des Abendlandes*—the "decline of the West" made famous in the 1920s by Oswald Spengler. Even Edward Gibbon interrupted his *History of the Decline and Fall of the Roman Empire* to insert a chapter reassuring his readers why it would not occur again.

The explanations are many: overextension, barbarian incursions, even, for the Roman Empire, the coming of Christianity. We are struck by the sublime but broken and marred statues from classical antiquity, failing to realize that they were in most cases deliberately defaced by the Christians.

I have in front of me a copy of William Bell Dinsmoor's *Architecture of Ancient Greece*, a primer I used when studying classical archaeology at Oxford. One chapter is entitled "The Beginning of the Decadence." He is talking not about the collapse of Greco-Roman civilization in the fifth and sixth centuries AD, but about the decline in Greek architecture from its zenith in the fifth century BC—the Golden Age—to the period following it. The Greeks and Romans continued to build grand and magnificent temples for centuries after this supposed beginning of the decadence.

Nonetheless, the fourth century BC, says Dinsmoor, "is characterised by certain general tendencies," notably "the decline of aesthetic perfection" from the zenith represented by the Parthenon, built the century before.

It is almost impossible to avoid seeing the development of Greek architecture this way. The temples built in the sixth century BC and earlier seem crude and ungainly compared to the masterworks on the Athenian Acropolis, just as later constructions, often even more magnificent, seem overdone and fussy.

These reflections may tell us something about the nature of creativity. To some extent I speak of the games of life metaphorically, but creativity is closer to an actual game than most of the rest. It presupposes a finite set of rules, dictated by the art form and medium in question, which present a wide but nevertheless limited display of versatility. There seems to an initial period in which these forms are learned or developed, a period of flourishing, and a period of decline. Usually the period of flourishing is short—not more than a generation or two—although the other two phases may vary greatly in length.

To view this process in a simpler light, we can look into the playroom. A small child has a set of blocks, such as Legos. Initially she learns how they fit together; then she learns what more beautiful and elaborate forms she can build. The forms are not the aim; it is the building. When she has finished something to her satisfaction, she knocks it down and starts over again. (I wonder if this is not the key to the rise and fall of civilizations.) When she has done as much as she can with the set she has, she loses interest and goes on to something else.

Adults with access to virtually limitless supplies of such blocks can work wonders. You can go online and find astonishing sculptures of huge animals, ships, and cities built with Legos. But the typical child does not have access to any such supply, so the variations available to her are much more limited, and consequently her interest is as well.

We can see a similar process with the ancient Greek temple, with its relatively standardized parts: columns, pediments, stylobates, architraves, and the rest. This form gives rise to a certain number of possibilities, but rather constricted ones. Typically, there are only three orders for the capitals at the top of columns: Doric, Ionic, and Corinthian. Each of these has its uses and intended effects, but they are circumscribed. Over the centuries, the ancient architects seem to have played out all of the possibilities before paganism was supplanted by a new religion that imposed its own rules for its sacred spaces.

A more recent example of such standardization is the Hollywood script for feature films, which is almost unbelievably formulaic, even down to the format. "Use the right font," counsels Christopher Riley in *The Hollywood Standard*. "Use some form of Courier, New Courier, or Courier Final Draft . . . Always use 12-point type.

Don't cheat. People who stare at scripts for a living will know. And they'll turn your script into a coffee cup." Why? "Over the years, a rule of thumb developed among filmmakers that one script page" formatted this way "translated, on average, to one minute of finished film."

The script must be generally between ninety and 120 pages, because that is the length of the standard film; a movie must offer something extraordinary to deserve any greater length.

There are three acts: the setup, the development of the plot, and the dénouement—a structure that goes back to Aristotle's *Poetics*, which I have heard cited in every screenwriting workshop I have attended.

Certain things must have happened in the script by or on page 5; certain other things must have happened by or on page 25. In his influential book from 2005, *Save the Cat! The Last Book on Screenwriting You'll Ever Need*, Blake Snyder talks about the "break into two," that is, Act Two:

It happens on page 25. I have been in many arguments. Why not page 28? What's wrong with 30? Don't. Please.

In a 110 page screenplay, it happens no later than 25.

Page 25 is the place where I always go first in a screenplay someone has handed me (we all have our reading quirks) to see "what happens on page 25." I want to know if 1) if anything happens and 2) if the screenwriter knows that something *should* happen. And I mean something big.

Because that's what is supposed to happen . . . on page 25. . . .

The act break is the moment where we leave the old world, the thesis statement, behind and proceed into a world that is the upside down version of that, its antithesis. But because these two worlds are so distinct, the act of actually stepping into Act Two must be definite.

These rules are well known among scriptwriters, who recognize that it is death for their projects to violate them. They have been set out in any number of scriptwriting books, going back at least to Syd Field's *Screenplay: The Foundations of Scriptwriting*, which was first published in 1979.

Snyder structures his script format into fifteen steps or "beats." You hardly need to have seen many movies to recognize such beats as "Bad Guys Close In," "All Is Lost," and "Dark Night of the Soul." "Dark Night of the Soul" shows the hero isolated and despondent. Often we see him guzzling whiskey (why it always has to be whiskey, I do not know)—always straight and usually out of the bottle.

The title *Save the Cat!* has to do with our sympathy for the hero. Sometimes a difficult, surly loner, sometimes a cool but snarky hipster, he must be shown very early as possessing an innate decency that will make the viewer root for him despite his defects. As Snyder puts it, "It's the scene where we meet the hero and the hero does something—like saving a cat—that defines who he and makes us, the audience, like him." The hero of the typical cop film, for example, is often a single dad, a widower raising a child whom he loves very much. Sometimes he is divorced, but in these cases we are usually led to understand that he is still in love with his ex-wife (although, in all my experience, I have never met anyone who was still in love with his ex-wife).

Recently I watched the 2019 film *In the Shadow of the Moon*, which portrays exactly this situation. Although it is ultimately a science fiction movie about time travel (a favorite these days), the first half replicates every cliché of every cop-buddy movie down the line. For example, the buddy must be shot at some point, so that for the hero, searching for the culprit is no longer a job but a matter of revenge.

We could go through similar exercises for the romantic comedy or rom-com, the coming-of-age movie, the action film, even the quirky indie film about misfits. There is no need to, of course: at this point you could practically write the scripts yourself.

Hollywood studios make many films these days, but they only film the same six different plots over and over. They have managed to survive partly through ingenious variations on basic themes (Snyder's "Give me the same thing . . . only different!") and especially magnificent special effects. As a rule, when a dramatic tradition is in decline, it relies more and more on special effects. This was as true on the ancient Athenian stage as it is for Twentieth Century Fox.

Although the Hollywood feature film has become formulaic, we need to consider the role of formula in mass culture. You rarely go to a fast-food restaurant in the hopes of culinary discovery: usually you know exactly what you want. You *want* a standardized product: not only French fries, but French fries made exactly the same way you had them last time. Similarly, you never watch a rom-com wondering whether the man and woman will get together in the end; it is just a matter of seeing how they overcome the many obstacles presented to them (a common one being that they cannot stand the sight of each other at first). But you went to the rom-com expecting that. Probably for this reason, these movies are popular on dates.

Creativity appears to thrive best when it is set within a definite but flexible structure. But this structure admits only so many possibilities, and it admits very few possibilities on the highest level: there is only one Parthenon. As the themes are reworked and over-worked, the art form loses its power and is eventually discarded. Today the greatest creativity in American film is displayed not in the standard feature but in streamed television series, starting with *Sex and the City* and *The Sopranos* in the late 1990s.

A rigorous form—whether it is Dante's *terza rima* or the classic French tragedy of Corneille and Racine—becomes a kind of collaborator. When the form is looser, that structural support is weaker. Since the revolution in English-language poetry sparked by Ezra Pound's "Make It New!" movement in 1914, traditional verse forms—the sonnet, the villanelle—have fallen into the background. More poems are written, but arguably fewer of them are great poems. Some have observed that poetry anthologies from the nineteenth century and earlier feature a relatively small number of authors. A modern anthology, on the other hand, generally contains only one or two poems by the same poet. Possibly because the old forms were more difficult: they enabled a very few to attain mastery, abandoning practically all the others to doggerel. Poets today have a freer hand, but this relative lack of discipline makes excellence that much more difficult.

Part of this trend is explained by the often-remarked poverty of rhymes in the English language, which can give rhymed verse the weakness of monotony. If you look at Dryden's translation of the *Aeneid*, written in rhymed heroic couplets, you will notice exasperatingly fast that practically every page has a line ending with "fate," followed in the next line by one of the few words that rhyme with it. Even in the greatest master of the rhymed heroic couplet, Alexander Pope, rhyme makes the verse seem strangely facile (although writing it was no doubt anything but). In his preface to *Paradise Lost*, Milton writes:

> The measure is English heroic verse, without rhyme, as that of Homer in Greek and Virgil in Latin; rhyme being no necessary adjunct or true ornament of poem or good verse, in longer works especially, but the invention of a barbarous age, to set off wretched matter and lame metre; graced, indeed, since by the use of some famous modern poets, carried away by custom, but much to their vexation, hindrance, and constraint, to express many things otherwise, and for the most part worse than else they would have expressed them.

Rhyme in English often descends into the "jingling sound of like endings," as Milton puts it. It is not a coincidence that the greatest masters of English poetry—Milton as well as Shakespeare—wrote for the most part in unrhymed blank verse, a meter that is regular and harmonious, but enough in keeping with the rhythms of English speech to be flexible and expressive.

Nevertheless, even an extremely loose art form has its limits and restraints, beyond which vitality degenerates into hackwork. Abstract expressionism in painting, centered in post–World War II New York—was explosive in its day. Although people joked, "My kid could do that," there is a power in the great Jackson Pollock canavases that is hard to escape or deride. Even here, the vigor of the movement exhausted itself in the first generation. Many abstract expressionist paintings are still made, but very few display real vitality or ingenuity: they can sit in the conference rooms of corporations, where they are comfortably ignored.

Not all instances of artistic decline have to do with hitting the limits of a genre. The Great American Novel is not a myth: there are many examples. Most of them center on themes of solitude and isolation, sometimes contented, sometimes tormented: James Fenimore Cooper's Hawkeye, tramping through the forests of New York state during the French and Indian War; crazy Ahab on the *Pequod*; Huck and Jim floating on a raft down the Mississippi; Jay Gatsby pining alone in his ostentatious mansion. The sense of isolation even persists when the character is firmly embedded in a society: the guilt-gnawed Arthur Dimmesdale in Puritan Boston; John P. Marquand's George Apley in a Boston two and a half centuries later; Henry James's solipsistic neurotics among the American émigrés of the Gilded Age.

With or without this theme, the American novel retained its vitality through the 1960s but lost it rapidly thereafter. I have read very few American novels of the last half century, even the best, that did not reek of self-indulgence. One example is Jennifer Egan's *Visit from the Goon Squad*, which won the Pulitzer Prize in 2011. I gave up reading Thomas Pynchon's *Vineland* halfway through, tired of seeing yet another northern California eccentric introduced every page or two. I got ninety pages into David Foster Wallace's *Infinite Jest*, which was very funny, but I did not expect that another 910 pages of the same jokes would continue to be as amusing. Creative vitality in fiction has been displaced onto the present-day graphic novel, the offspring of the wild underground comics of the sixties and seventies.

Write it off to my own idiosyncratic tastes, but I think it is fair to say that there are no novelists today that attract the American imagination as Fitzgerald, Faulkner, and Hemingway did less than a century ago.

The lifelessness and superficiality of the current American literary novel cannot be because it has reached the technical limits of what is a very broad and accepting genre, but because, one senses, of some larger social vitiation: a masturbatory self-obsession has supplanted great themes and vistas. Philip Roth is considered one of the greatest novelists of this era, but he is a prime instance of this self-obsession, which he transcends only rarely, as in *The Human Stain*. I am reminded of Havelock Ellis's remark that a civilization can no more be blamed for decadence than a flower can be blamed for going to seed.

The greatest artistic achievements, then, require two things: the seed of an individual genius and the field of a genre that can accommodate that genius. An artwork—a painting, a tragedy, a building—may be largely an individual creation, but the genre is almost invariably a collective construction. Here is Aristotle's account of the birth of tragedy:

> It certainly began in improvisations—as did also comedy; the one originating with the authors of the dithyramb, the other with those of the phallic songs, which still survive as institutions in many of our cities. And its advance after that was little by little, through *their improving on whatever they had before them at each stage*. It was in fact only *after a long series of changes that the movement of tragedy stopped on its attaining to its natural form*. The number of actors was first increased to two by Aeschylus, who curtailed the business of the Chorus, and

made the dialogue take the leading part in the play.

A third actor and scenery were due to Sophocles.

Tragedy acquired also its magnitude.

Notice that each contributor added something new until tragedy attained to "its natural form," after which it stopped changing. Here again we have the evolution of a genre, its maturity, and its eventual decline, as the "natural form" only admits a certain finite number of creative possibilities before becoming stale and uninteresting.

Then there are the majestic achievements that can only be collectively accomplished—any work, really, of architecture or engineering.

All this said, it would be foolish to limit our concept of creativity to artworks of the first rank. I am convinced that cooking is one of the highest of the arts, although it is not usually recognized as such because its creations are so ephemeral. You may hear a Beethoven quartet more or less as he intended it, but you will never taste the culinary achievements of a chef of his era.

The present age is devising art forms of its own, inspiring new types of creativity. Some are games. In *The New York Times*, Melissa Kirsch writes that the role playing game Dungeons & Dragons is a matter of "imagining and then inhabiting characters, writing stories collaboratively, escaping reality while developing real-life social skills. . . . Rules govern interactions, and a dungeon master who acts as both narrator and referee enforces them. In the safety of this container, players explore, improvise, cocreate worlds."

Video games, computerized descendants of Dungeons & Dragons, are another nascent art genre. Whether they will ever attain a "natural form" that fosters true greatness remains to be seen, but then Aristotle pointed out that tragedy has its roots in the crude dithyrambs (reveling songs) and phallic songs of the populace. I am in no way a fan of hip-hop, but I have listened to it more than once and wondered if the future of American poetry lies here.

I could go further and suggest that the most impressive creative achievements of the future might not be recognizable to us today. After all, the most admired invention of the twenty-first century so far is the smartphone: what would people centuries ago have made of it?

One area in which everyone demonstrates creativity, or a lack of it, is personal style. In his book *Uncertain Places*, my friend Mitch Horowitz writes,

Are you dressing as you wish? When you get up in the morning—whether it is a weekday, workday, weekend, or vacation—are you comporting yourself in a way that feels natural? How *exactly* do you want to dress in the world? How do you want to wear your hair? How do you want to wear your makeup? What image, what persona, do you feel most comfortable projecting? Do not get lost in thinking that I am just talking about the outer shell of things. Again, I believe in no difference, finally, between the kernel and the shell. It is one great interplay. You are given the gift, as a co-creator, of crafting your image, and it will reverberate through your entire being.

Citing Claude Bristol, an author from the 1930s, Horowitz observes, "In addition to Gandhi's political, diplomatic, and ethical genius, he also cultivated a definite image. His walking stick, sandals, spectacles, cropped hair, and traditional robe came from the so-called lower rungs of the caste system in India. His adoption of that appearance is part of what made him into a colossus on the world stage."

Other figures bear out this claim: Lincoln with his moustacheless beard and stovepipe hat, FDR with his jaunty cigarette holder, Churchill with his cigar and Homburg hat. Contrast these great figures with the world leaders of today: Joe Biden, Boris Johnson, Emmanuel Macron, Vladimir Putin, and Xi Jinping, for all their differences, wear the same dark blue suit that has become the world's standard uniform for chief executives. Their identical dress leads the conspiratorial part of the mind to suppose that they are all employees of the same world-dominating cabal. A more plausible explanation appears in John T. Molloy's *Dress for Success* from the 1980s, which says, "Suits that give you the most credibility with the upper middle class are dark blue and dark gray solids and pinstripes in both colors. . . . Only the dark blue solid will give you credibility with the lower middle class." When you have little inside yourself to express, go with the safe bet: dark blue.

"You can fashion a uniform, too," Horowitz continues, "so that every day you look your best, you are at ease and relaxed, you project the image you want, and you can dress daily and pack for travel with minimum effort. For me, it is t-shirts, leather boots, black jeans, and leather jackets. It is who I am. It is easy. It is versatile."

Indeed this outfit, coupled with his tattoos and tall, well-muscled frame, give Horowitz a powerful air of hip urban machismo. He adds, *"more doors opened when I gravitated toward an appearance that I found self-expressive."*

I too dress in a fashion I find comfortable, although it is much more conservative—business casual. No doubt I dress like a Connecticut preppie because I *am* a

Connecticut preppie. In any case, it is a sensible choice for my age: men in their midsixties generally do not do well with style innovations.

Many, perhaps, most people do not express themselves in their dress—or if they do, they are expressing an inner vacuity. I live in the western suburbs of Chicago, a chiefly white, middle-class area. People here go everywhere as if they were dressed for mowing the lawn: baseball caps, sweatshirts, jeans, sneakers. I went to a memorial service a few years back where most of those present dressed that way—even and especially the older ones.

Styles that appeal to younger people—goth, gangsta, fashionista, hippie—may be representing not their true identities, but a search for one. It is part of the growth process. We all have to try on a few personas before we get it right.

All four of the previous games can be played satisfactorily by going no further than the point of adequacy. Success at survival means having enough income to pay for the necessities of life and a few of the luxuries. Love: most people are satisfied (rightly) with a devoted spouse and children and a solid network of friends. Power: some degree of freedom from political despotism and the subtler tyrannies of the workplace and society as well as the capacity to direct one's life as one wishes. And we all take our pleasures where we can. Indeed going past adequacy in these arenas can lead to excess and ruin.

Creativity is different. I strongly suspect that in order to live the fullest and happiest life, an individual has to excel creatively—to achieve mastery—in some realm of life. Human civilization offers the broadest vista of possibilities: cake decorating, fly fishing, nephrology, haircutting, real estate law. I believe every person is happiest when he or she reaches the peak of achievement in some area. Ideally it comes with a profession, which enables one to make a living—and in most areas, mastery means more renown and better pay. But not always: an old Kabbalist I knew used to say, "Creativity is for pleasure, not for profit."

We can look at mastery in three basic stages. The first level is that of the trainee: learning what you need to know to practice your craft. It can be extremely brief: in Massachusetts, for example, you are licensed to sell insurance by taking a one-day course and passing an easy exam. For a surgeon, it means years in residency.

The next stage is one of practice. If you are selling insurance, you have to go out and find clients, listen to them, and tailor the policies they buy to their specific needs. Or you have learned the basics of carpentry well enough that somebody will pay you to do it. At first you are only suited to simple tasks, ideally in the context of a larger project that will help you expand your abilities.

The final stage is mastery. You have learned the skills and tricks of your craft to the point where you can not only work independently but can create and execute plans and train others. If you attain enough mastery, you will carry out your tasks with a speed, confidence, and excellence that may amaze others. A story by the Chinese sage Chuang-tzu (or Zhuangzi) tells of a cook who knows how to carve up a cow with supreme expertise. He says, "The average cook goes through a knife every month, because he hacks and chops. A good cook changes knives once a year, because he merely chops but doesn't hack. Because I neither hack nor chop, I've used this same knife for nineteen years, and it's still like new."

These three stages still exist in present-day crafts. Here is a definition of how they apply to electricians: "An apprentice is a beginner or trainee who works under direct supervision of a master electrician. A journeyman is trained and experienced and can work on his own under the general guidance of a master. A master originates projects, gets permits for construction and installations and oversees the work of journeymen and apprentices." These specifications form part of the National Electrical Code in the U.S., which is used by all states in licensing electricians.

These stages correspond to the three levels of Blue Lodge Freemasonry: Entered Apprentice, Fellow Craft, and Master Mason, levels which are attained by undergoing certain initiation rituals in a Masonic lodge (I am not a Mason and cannot speak of the process firsthand). These rites appear to go back to medieval times, when Masonry was still an operative craft that worked on stone: "speculative Masonry," which uses the terms and concepts of the masonic craft to express esoteric teachings, only came into being centuries later.

The late philosopher Peter Lamborn Wilson, writing under the pseudonym Hakim Bey, said that "being itself is in a state of chaos, & that life is free to generate its own spontaneous orders. . . . *the generosity of being IS becoming.*" He points toward the boundless creativity of reality: "If I wanted to be fancy I could call this nothing the Abyss . . . or even god." Whether we choose to call it God, Chaos, the Abyss, the Source, or the universe, we as humans are the children of this boundless ground of being. So we too have the same urge to create, to make new. Creativity brings us close to our own center, which is boundless vitality. Hence the need for creative mastery.

This mastery is not the same as the Master Game, although it can be seen as a prelude to it. We have one more game to explore first.

# 6

# Courage

I am standing in a darkened museum gallery in Manassas, Virginia. In front of me is a large map of the vicinity. If you press a button, lines of lights will start to flash, some blue, some orange. They outline the First Battle of Bull Run (as known to the Federals; the Confederates called it the First Battle of Manassas) in July 1861. The blue lights indicate the movements of the Federal troops, the orange lights those of the Confederates. An accompanying six-minute film narrates the course of the battle.

The lights move around, often very rapidly, back and forth. But one string of orange lights barely moves at all. It represents the brigade commanded by Thomas J. Jackson. Unlike most of the other Confederates, who were breaking and running, Jackson's troops held firm until reinforcements under General Joseph Johnston could relieve them, reversing the course of the day. The Federal troops fled in disarray, ending the first major battle of the Civil War.

Jackson's performance on that day gave him the nickname by which history came to know him: Stonewall Jackson. I knew a few things about Jackson, but not enough to give me a full picture of this enigmatic man, so I read S.C. Gwynne's *Rebel Yell: The Violence, Passion, and Redemption of Stonewall Jackson*. Despite its rhetoric, peculiar to Civil War books (chapters have titles like "The Bullet's Song" and "A Jagged Line of Blood"), it is an exhaustive and absorbing biography. After reading it, I did not exactly feel that I understood Jackson—indeed I wonder if anyone ever did—although I understood him more than I had.

Jackson's chief feature was an almost superhuman courage in battle. As a recent West Point graduate, he distinguished himself in the Mexican War in 1846–48. Then, enduring the ennui that peace imposes on the professional soldier, he took a job teaching science at the Virginia Military Institute, where he was generally acknowledged to be the worst instructor—lumbering, awkward, and (curiously, in the light of later events) oblivious to the misbehavior of his students.

When the Civil War broke out, Jackson, like most Virginians, took his stand with the Confederacy, beginning perhaps the most impressive military career of that convulsive war. After distinguishing himself at Manassas, he led a brilliant campaign against much larger Union forces in Virginia's Shenandoah Valley, followed by further triumphs.

Jackson's successes were due in part to a willingness to drive his troops relentlessly. In one campaign, writes Gwynne, "Jackson had forced his men to walk more than one hundred miles through a succession of brutal winter storms, high winds, ice, mud, and temperature that stayed well below freezing. In spite of repeated protests by his officers, conditions that worsened as they march, and troops with frozen, bleeding, bare feet, he held fast to his objective."

He also had enormous capacity for surprise. He rarely took even his closest advisors into his confidence, issuing orders that his troops did not understand, forcing them to unknown destinations, for reasons they were never told. Usually these marches ended in an attack (almost always successful) on Federal forces of superior strength, to be followed by a vigorous pursuit.

Jackson's men cursed him at times, but they were devoted to him, and his victories endeared him not only to his troops but to the Confederate populace, who by 1862 were beginning to suspect that their grand scheme of secession might not have been such a great idea after all and welcomed any cheering news.

Like most great men of history, Jackson was a man of puzzles and contradictions. He was frequently petty and vindictive toward subordinates who did not measure up to his own peculiar standards of duty (permitting themselves, for example, to be defeated by the enemy), but genial to friends, tender and affectionate toward his family, and rigorously adamant about personal courtesy. In battle, he was often not only valiant but joyful: writing about the Battle of Chancellorsville in May 1863, a fellow officer said, "I well remember the elation of Jackson. He seemed full of life & joy. His whole demeanor was cheerful and lively compared with his usual quiet manner."

These paradoxes centered around Jackson's strong religious faith. A devout Presbyterian, he prayed constantly. In his last days, he chatted with friends about "how every aspect of a man's religious life should be a self-conscious religious act. While washing oneself, one might imagine the cleansing blood of Christ; while dressing, one might pray to be cloaked in the Savior's righteousness; while eating, to be feeding on the bread of heaven. Jackson had long lived this way, consecrating even his most trivial actions to God," writes Gwynne.

Jackson read his Bible devotedly and took inspiration from the battles in the Old Testament. "Joshua's battle with the Amalekites," he observes, "has clearness, brevity, fairness, modesty, and it traces the victory to its right source—the blessing of God." Indeed when Confederate papers praised him for his victories, he worried that their failure to attribute the victory to God might lead to the incipient nation's downfall. "Let our Government acknowledge the God of the Bible as its God, and we may expect soon to be a happy and independent people," he contended.

The Presbyterian element no doubt explains Jackson's courage in the face of danger. He applied the Calvinist notion of predestination not only to the next life but to this one: if God has carved out a destiny for everyone in eternity, no doubt he has done so on earth as well.

Jackson's courage was rooted in his conviction that he would be safe until the Lord chose to take him—an attitude that worked exactly up to the point where it didn't. At the battle of Chancellorsville, Jackson and some fellow officers, including A.P. Hill, another distinguished Confederate general, were fired upon by troops who mistook them in the dark for Federal horsemen. Hill saved himself by dropping on the ground, but Jackson was hit by three bullets, including two that shattered his left arm.

Jackson was carried to safety, and his arm amputated. He seemed to be recovering but caught pneumonia and died a few days later. Jackson, always protected by Providence from the enemy's assaults, was killed by friendly fire (one of many ironic terms inspired by the logic of war). At the end, he fell into a delirium, issuing orders to imaginary units, then grew calm. A smile of "ineffable sweetness" passed across his face. His last words were, "Let us cross over the river and rest under the shade of the trees."

Extreme cases of courage are rarely devoid of cruelty, as Jackson showed. He was outraged by the way the Federal troops treated his beloved Virginia, but he made it clear that he would have done much worse if he had gotten his hands on Baltimore or Philadelphia. In one exchange with Hunter McGuire, his medical staff director, he said, "'How horrible is war.'

"'Horrible, yes,' McGuire replied. 'But we have been invaded, so what can we do?'

"'Kill them, sir,' said Jackson. 'Kill them all.'"

It may require courage to go into battle, but when in it, men frequently transform. Gwynne writes about one point at the Battle of Antietam in 1862: "There was something fearless and primitive and elemental in the combat that morning, a kind of madness or possession, as soldiers left their humanity behind and became mere feral killing machines."

We like to pretend that humanity consists of kindness and love, but perhaps this assessment is too gentle. Cruelty is just as much a part of us and is often more in evidence. Simone Weil saw this as the central characteristic of the *Iliad*:

The true hero, the true subject, the centre of the *Iliad*, is force. Force employed by man, force that enslaves man, force before which man's flesh shrinks away. In this work, at all times, the human spirit is shown as modified by its relations with force, as swept away, blinded, by the very force it imagined it could handle, as deformed by the weight of the force it submits to.

Weil goes on to say:

The strong are, as a matter of fact, never absolutely strong, nor are the weak absolutely weak, but neither is aware of this. They have in common a refusal to believe that they both belong to the same species: the weak see no relation between themselves and the strong, and vice versa. . . .

A moderate use of force, which alone would enable man to escape being enmeshed in its machinery, would require superhuman virtue, which is as rare as dignity in weakness.

Moreover, moderation itself is not without its perils, since prestige, from which force derives at least three quarters of its strength, rests principally upon that marvelous indifference that the strong feel toward the weak, an indifference so contagious that it infects the very people who are the objects of it. Yet ordinarily excess is not arrived at through prudence or politic considerations. On the contrary, man dashes to it as to an irresistible temptation.

Is courage, then, an admirable victory over fear? ("Never take counsel of your fears," said Jackson.) Or is it the unstripping of the veneer of tenderness imposed by civilization, unleashing a bottomless inner violence?

Some have contended that Weil misunderstood the *Iliad*, but it seems to me that she understood it all too well.

For Aristotle, courage, like all virtues, is a mean—a moderation between two extremes, in this case recklessness and cowardice. Courage does not consist of fearlessness in all circumstances: "We would say someone is mad, or insensible, if he feared nothing, neither earthquakes nor waves, as is said of the Celts." "Nor," he adds, "would we consider a man a coward if he feared outrage toward his wife and children, or envy, or any such things."

For Aristotle, the ultimate nature of courage (as with all things) has to do with its end or aim. "Each thing is defined by its end. The courageous man stands firm and does brave things on account of what is noble." And what is noble? "A man is properly called brave if he is fearless of a noble death, and of such emergencies as lead to death: and these are especially have to do with war. . . . They are brave for whom there is prowess or it is noble to die."

The warrior still stands as the personification of courage, and (ideally at least) the warrior lives by a certain ethos. This was true in classical antiquity: the Homeric heroes lived by the code of their time. It was nothing like today's. The quarrel that begins the *Iliad* takes place because Agamemnon has taken away Achilles' slave girl Briseis. This is an outrage, because she is Achilles' rightful property as spoils of war. Nowhere is there any question about the underlying rule, no qualms about enslaving human captives. It is taken as the natural state of affairs.

Christianity, centered around principles of mildness, greeted the moral dilemmas of war with more ambivalence, but it soon faced the realization that war was inevitable in many instances. The medieval church dealt with this problem by establishing the famous code of chivalry. Today chivalry has all sorts of meanings (holding open the door for a lady), but let's see what it was in essence. Here is one version of the code of chivalry from medieval France:

I. Thou shalt believe all that the Church teaches, and shalt observe all its directions.

II. Thou shalt defend the Church.

III. Thou shalt defend all weaknesses, and constitute thyself the defender of them.

IV. Thou shalt love the country in which thou wast born.

V. Thou shalt not recoil from thine enemy.

VI. Thou shalt make war against the Infidel without cessation, and without mercy.

VII. Thou shalt perform scrupulously thy feudal duties, if they be not contrary to the law of God.

VIII. Thou shalt never lie, and shalt remain faithful to thy pledged word.

IX. Thou shalt be generous, and give largesse to everyone.

X. Thou shalt everywhere and always be the champion of the Right and the Good against Injustice and Evil.

These rules reveal their context: an era in which fidelity to the Catholic church and a vehement opposition to infidels (meaning Muslims) were central features of the military ethos.

I found something strangely comforting in reading these rules, although I could never follow them myself. A knight who swore fidelity to them would have guidelines for action in almost all cases. He would have a firm and rigorous sense of right and wrong.

The ancient Hindu *Laws of Manu* set out its own rules for the behavior of a *kshatriya* (warrior):

One should not, fighting in battle, slay enemies by concealed weapons, nor with barbed or poisoned (weapons), nor with fire-kindled arrows.

Nor should one (mounted) slay an enemy down on the ground, a eunuch, a suppliant, one with loosened hair, one seated, one who says, "I am thy (prisoner);"

Nor one asleep, one without armor, one naked, one without weapons, one not fighting, a looker-on, one engaged with another;

Nor one who has his arms broken, a distressed man, one badly hit, one afraid, one who has fled; remembering (virtue), one should not slay them.

Today such a code is hard to find anywhere, leaving a widely felt void. One remarkable illustration occurs in Jim Jarmusch's 1999 film *Ghost Dog*. The title character, played by Forest Whittaker, is a loner who has resolved to live by the samurai code as expressed in the seventeenth-century Japanese book *Hagakure*. A samurai must have a master to serve, and for Ghost Dog, that is Louie, a Mafioso, who does not understand his peculiar ethos but recognizes his usefulness as a hired killer. The film illustrates the weird beauty of this ideal as well as its total unsuitability for present-day America.

Islam does enjoin holy war—*jihad*—in certain cases, but like the crusader code, it traditionally holds to a certain ethical standard. The Muslim writer Abul Khatib writes:

> On the basis of the Qur'an and Sunnah, Muslim jurists enunciated rules that forbade Muslims to kill noncombatants. There were explicit stipulations that the aged, the young, and women must not be killed or molested in any way. Places of worship must not be destroyed, nor must any harm be done to monks, worshippers, or seekers of God of any kind. Fruit trees must not be cut, and harvests must not be set on fire. Even animals were not to be killed in the pursuit of *jihad*.

I do not know how present-day terrorists justify their actions in light of such ideas.

Muslims also cite a *hadith* (saying) of the prophet Muhammad. When some mujaheddin were returning from a raid against unbelievers, the Prophet said, "Welcome to those who have finished the lesser jihad. The greater *jihad*, however, remains to them." Asked what he meant, the prophet explained, "It is the *jihad* against one's self, the *nafs*."

Similarly, Orthodox Christianity has the concept of "unseen warfare," in which the aspirant struggles, not against flesh and blood, but against his own negative impulses and habits, which the tradition calls "passions."

The true warrior is not like most people. Something inside motivates him in a way that the rest of us find incomprehensible. Jim Morris, a Special Forces paratrooper in Vietnam, observes:

A parachute jump or a firefight blows you into another plane of experience. Colors are brighter, time slows, sound fades, and you're making connections faster than ever before. But you're not making decisions. You're on autopilot. All those decisions were made in a thousand practice sessions. No one is what you would properly call sane in such a situation. You might pursue an action that allows you to survive and find yourself in a courtroom a month later, with a prosecutor who accuses you of having acted unreasonably.

Reason is not the issue. The reason part of your brain is paralyzed. The lizard brain is what's happening.

On the other hand, you're as close to death as you're ever going to be, and it's just glorious. I'm convinced that's what the ancients were talking about when they spoke of the glory of war, the adrenaline rush that gets you through it.

Morris continues:

I believe most masculine activities are designed to reproduce this feeling, or a fraction of it, in a relatively safe environment. I'm convinced that this is what the "glory of war" is about, not the conquests, nor the booty, nor the women, nor the medals, but the actual down-in-the-mud hacking and hewing with sword and mace, while the adrenaline blows you into an entirely different plane of consciousness.

Men are hardwired for this, and today most of them don't even know it. They seem lost.

This passage is like a lens that suddenly brings a great number of things into focus. It all becomes clear, the whole gamut—athletics, mountain climbing, daredevil feats, as well as more humdrum (and dangerous) versions, such as highway speeding, prodigious drinking, and acts of crime. They are unconscious replacements for the raw ecstasies of fighting and killing. Morris sometimes seems to regret the loss of these primal pleasures (modern men, deprived of the primal battle, "seem lost"), but if we had not managed to put a damper on them, we would not have civilization in its present form.

Those who love war—the Stonewall Jacksons of humanity—no doubt feel such thrills. But the courage game, idealized as the way of the warrior, is, at its most sublime, beyond the adrenaline rush.

An updated version of the warrior ideal was published in 1991 in *Gnosis*, a journal of the Western mystical traditions, of which I was then the editor. When the Gulf War broke out at the beginning of the year, we decided to devote an issue to the paradoxical concept of holy war.

One submission struck me in particular. It came in under the title of "Peaceful Warriors—Hah!" and I would have liked to run it that way, but I was overruled, so the article ended up being entitled "No Peaceful Warriors!" It was a response to Dan Millman's popular book *The Way of the Peaceful Warrior*, a concept that the author of this article regarded as a contradiction in terms.

The author of "No Peaceful Warriors!" is Ambrose Hollingworth Redmoon, a mysterious figure whose accomplishments (says his writer's credit) include writing a military unit tactics manual and serving as occult editor on the original staff of *Rolling Stone* magazine. At the article's beginning, he identifies himself as "a real, live, initiated, trained, experienced, traditional, hereditary warrior with thirty-seven body scars and a trophy or two on my belt."

For Redmoon, a warrior has to do with war—in the literal sense. "The warrior's quest is for the throat of the enemy." Furthermore, "like all paths of initiation, that of the warrior begins on that level claimed by some ignorant ones to be only an illusion, and by others, equally ignorant, to be the only reality: the plane of dense matter, the world of form." The initiation is "physical encounter with the enemy. There is no . . . spiritual warrior who is not a physical warrior first."

Who is the enemy?

Those . . . who with a clear consciousness and immense power enjoy the full exercise of their will at the expense of others. Sadistic greed is combined with a clear, intelligent mind and a tough, powerful, fast physique, all in a person who is quite beyond the reach of "consciousness lifting." Such people are not confused, they are not victims, they are not seeking. They are not cowards, most of them. They are going to abuse, terrify, and possess because they find it efficient and enjoyable. There is also another type, an unpredictable idiot fringe, where most of the weirdos, exhibitionists, sneaks, and thrill-seekers are to be found. These latter squabble over the leavings after the previous types eat a few "peaceful warriors" for breakfast.

It would be difficult to contend that such types do not exist or that they do not exercise great influence.

The true warrior, Redmoon argues, "a protector, preserver, and a destroyer, not a conqueror. He destroys the invader, the raper, the killer—the enemy. When there is no enemy, a soldier might contrive one; never the warrior."

The warrior "does not desire pretexts" for fighting.

Diplomacy is the first move of a response to conflict: even the imperial Roman legions always offered the olive branch first. After that a still-persistent enemy can often be dislocated and defeated by maneuver alone. But, dear gentle reader, the true warrior is ready to decide the issue by direct physical violence if the enemy refuses to desist otherwise.

The warrior's function is "to protect the weak, the home, the individual, the Mother. . . . He who abuses any woman abuses my mother." He goes on to say:

> I have no tolerance for wife beating; this is a crime second only to rape, which is a capital offense in my book. Men who beat women do so because they can. There is no good reason, no excuse. It is the responsibility of the protectors, both male and female, to prevent this and to help women become physically too dangerous for men to even try. . . . Court orders are extremely difficult for women to obtain in most areas. Physical force is considerably more available. *And it works.* (Emphasis Redmoon's)

Redmoon does not believe in the weakness of women: "You may have assumed that I presume a warrior to be masculine. Not so. There is no gender. I have fought shoulder-to-shoulder and back-to-back with women, and I am here to tell you that women and men are equally effective in combat. Men excel at packing ammo and bearing wounded. Women have a higher pain threshold."

The codes I have discussed above deal with war in its traditional sense: combat, often hand-to-hand. How do they apply to war as it has evolved (or devolved) over the past century? As Paul Fussell showed in his book *The Great War and Modern Memory*, the First World War, with its hideous carnage to capture a few yards of no-man's land and entire regiments wiped out in a single day, dashed the old lie of the nobility of war—as did the sheer and ruthless mechanization of the process (which continues to our own day: we can now kill the enemy with drones instead of troops.)

How would you behave in extreme circumstances? I cannot answer this question; I have wondered more than once what I would do myself. Only a fool would attempt to say without having been there. *Lord Jim* is about a man who imagined himself a hero but found otherwise in a moment of danger.

The British economist R.H. Tawney apparently had similar concerns before he went over the top at the Battle of the Somme in 1916. Here is how he felt after he did:

I had been worried by the thought: "Suppose one should lose one's head and get other men cut up! Suppose one's legs should take fright and refuse to move!" Now I knew it was all right. I shouldn't be frightened and I shouldn't lose my head. Imagine the joy of that discovery! I felt quite happy and self-possessed. It wasn't courage. That, I imagine, is the quality of facing danger which one knows to be danger, of making one's spirit triumph over the bestial desire to live in this body. But I knew that I was in no danger. I knew I shouldn't be hurt; knew it positively, much more positively than I know most things I'm paid for knowing.

Courage, of course, does not apply in the same way in all circumstances: someone may be fearless in one area and timid in another. Years ago, when I was teaching philosophy at a community college in western Massachusetts, I had a student; he was a veteran who had done three tours of duty in Iraq.

"That must have been intense," I said.

He shrugged. But he was terrified by the idea of going out on a first date.

It is almost a cliché: the decorated commando is a coward in the bedroom. Courage does not take the same form in all situations.

Although we are not usually on a quest for the throat of the enemy, life demands courage of us in countless smaller situations: asking the boss for a raise, asking a beautiful woman for a date, saying no in circumstances that involve no danger more acute than someone else's disappointment. More profound are the confrontations with one's own inner demons: the *nafs* of the Muslims and the "passions" of esoteric Christianity. Many battle-hardened veterans have come home to find that fighting the enemy was easier than facing their own posttraumatic stress disorder.

Then there are the nonviolent forms of courage: enduring indignities and dangers to stand up for what is right and to oppose injustice—virtues that many in modern society value more than courage in battle. It may not be a greater form of courage, but it is not an inferior one.

Many traditions hold that warriors who fulfill their destiny through death in battle receive a reward in the afterlife. The heavenly compensations of a faithful Muslim who dies fighting for the faith are well known. Only warriors slain in combat were to be admitted to Odin's Valhalla. The *Laws of Manu* say, "Kings who, desirous to slay one another, fight with their greatest strength in battles and without turning away, go to heaven."

What awaits us in the afterlife—which virtues are rewarded, which punished, which ignored—is up for guessing. Possibly, as I suggested in the prologue, the objective of the game of life has little or nothing to do with our beliefs about it, which are mere constructs invented to explain what we do not understand.

I have put this chapter next to last in this book because I suspect that the courage game is closest to the Master Game. For the most part, the other games are restricted to the circle that we know as life, but those who play the courage game—or some of them at any rate—may do so out of a hunch that there is something that is more important. Why else would they sacrifice their lives? Many do so accidentally, it is true, or out of fear of accusations of cowardice, or because of conditioning, or because they know that desertion in the face of the enemy means certain death and disgrace back home.

But I believe that at least a few who play the courage game do so because it points to values beyond life. This could be the case whether one dies by a warrior's code, for a principle, or for the sake of others: "Greater love hath no man than this, that a man lay down his life for his friends" (John 15:13). They all operate on the premise that these values are more important than one mere physical life.

Such a belief points toward an afterlife, or at any rate toward a realization that there is something immortal and indestructible in the human being that it is worth cultivating even at the expense of a physical life. Courage may not be the ultimate value, but it may be one that must be encountered and assimilated in order to achieve completeness of spirit. By such a view, one mere incarnation counts for little in such an equation.

My friend Ray Grasse has written a thought-provoking essay on life's tribulations entitled "Suffering and Soul Making on the Mean Streets of Planet Earth." He reminisces about a time in his childhood,

> when I watched two older gentlemen discussing their battlefield experiences back in World War II. It was almost as though they were trying to outdo each other with the hardships they endured and were practically bragging about the suffering they'd experienced. ("Yeah, but you should have seen what *I* went through at the Battle of the Bulge!") . . . We clearly dislike suffering and try to avoid it at all costs. Yet once we've gone through it, we'll sometimes look back on it with a certain pride at having survived it, wearing it almost like a badge of honor.

Ray adds: "I think this has something to tell us about the role and value of earthly existence itself, in terms of the role it plays in our spiritual evolution." He views this question in the course of many lifetimes: "as a result of having spent those thousands or perhaps millions of years down here on earth," one acquires "a quality not just of depth and complexity but also one of *compassion* and *empathy*, which can only come from having suffered and dealt with great struggle and resistance. That's because the soul grows its spiritual muscles by pushing up against obstacles, against resistance, and contending with 'friction.'"

It could be that the courage game—played even to the point of death—has some role of this kind in the development of the human spirit.

A peculiar angle on this possibility is found in Natalie Sudman's *Application of Impossible Things*, which describes a near-death experience (NDE) she underwent while a military contractor during the Iraq War. NDEs as a whole tend to be rather uniform: you can read dozens of them that resemble one another to the point of monotony. Hers was different.

Sudman was in a military vehicle that was exploded by a car bomb. Badly injured, she went into an altered state in which she found herself addressing what she calls the Gathering: a collection of thousands of beings from other dimensions and realities.

Through some psychic means, Sudman "presented what seems from my current physical body/conscious mind perception to be a transfer of information in the form of an inexplicably complex matrix. The information was minutely detailed and broadly conceptual—at once layered and infinitely dense, yet elegantly simple." This information, presented in a single gestalt, showed what life on the earthly plane was like in both conceptual and experiential terms. Her transgalactic audience was fascinated to learn what it was like to be blown up by a car bomb on earth—evidently a rare experience in the universe.

"I was aware that I deliberately offered the condensed data in fulfillment of a request that had been made by this Gathering of personalities prior to my taking on this body for this physical lifetime," she adds.

Sudman felt that this experience—tragic and painful from a conventional perspective, and one that left her partly disabled—was the reason she had been born. Indeed "what seemed quite elementary to me, being familiar with operating within a physical reality, was acknowledged as requiring a high degree of specialized skill from the perspective of those personalities at the Gathering." From the point of view of the universe as a whole, "*all of us* are sharing a unique experience that takes real and amazing skill."

What if the whole cavalcade of human experience—good, bad, joyous, excruciating, delightful, involving supreme acts of both atrocities and beneficence—has been constructed for such a purpose?

What if, bizarrely, death in battle is like a famous ride in an amusement park—something not to be missed at one point or another in a sequence of earthly lifetimes?

Appalling as this may seem, to push our thinking this far brings us to the Master Game.

# 7

# The Master Game

By now you may have wondered where religion fits into the games of life. Certainly it cannot be reduced to any single one of them, or to all six put together.

Marx's adage that religion is the opium of the people is often quoted, but rarely in its original context:

Religious suffering is, at one and the same time, the expression of real suffering and a protest against real suffering. Religion is the sigh of the oppressed creature, the heart of a heartless world, and the soul of soulless conditions. It is the *opium* of the people.

We need not follow Marx into atheism to see the truth of what he is saying. In its conventional forms, religion is a balm for the wounds inflicted by the six basic games of life. But it would not be so if it did not express a profound truth.

All religions are full of lies and delusions, yet in spite of these they survive. It is not that people are so easily taken in. It is that, beyond the lies and delusions, the religions all point to a fundamental and immutable fact—the immortality of the human spirit.

In terms of the Game of my prologue, religion reminds us that there is something beyond the Game. The game of life on earth is finite: it begins and ends, often apparently arbitrarily. People in ordinary life forget that there is something beyond: they are usually too submerged in whichever combination of the six games they happen to be playing. Perhaps that too is part of the Game: a reality beyond is posited, but it always seems remote, half hypothetical, possibly true but possibly not. Yet anyone who is certain that there is a life beyond the one we know—and they are many—cannot take the games of life too seriously.

Like religion, the Master Game is beyond the six other games. Like religion, it is concerned with another reality. It differs from religion in that it does not ask to be taken on faith: on the contrary, religious faith is often a major obstacle, particularly if it is infected with dogmatism, fanaticism, or any other types of false certainty.

The six games that we have already looked at are obligatory: you cannot go through life without playing them. Even the most cowardly soul has to face his fears sometime. Even the dullest man has to solve some problem, however basic, in a creative way. Even the coldest psychopath needs some warmth and affection, even if only in the form of an animal.

The Master Game imposes no such necessities. It may seem beside the point even to the best people. I mean those who go through life conscientiously, decently, with integrity, professionally accomplished and financially stable, with warm, loving families and many friends, and with a high reputation that is completely deserved. They may or not be informed by religious faith, but if they are, it is balanced and measured, free of excesses and fanaticism. Such people are in many ways enviable. They do not see anything missing in life. They have exempted themselves from the Master Game, and no one is wise enough to say they are wrong.

For other people, life does not offer enough. There are too many questions, too many missing pieces, too many things that are inexplicable. They realize that the conventional sources of wisdom—religious, philosophical, scientific—explain much less than they pretend to. These individuals have also found that the usual sources of gratification are not going to meet their needs. Indeed it is said that one prerequisite for the Master Game is to be *disappointed* in life. Often it takes some spectacular failure to be open to this game or even sense that it exists.

The Master Game has nothing to do with faith. It has to do with knowledge. In some cases, it begins with a realization. With G.I. Gurdjieff, we can call it "the sleep of man": "The chief feature of a modern man's being which explains *everything else that is lacking in him is sleep.* A modern man lives in sleep, in sleep he is born and in sleep he dies."

Gurdjieff is not talking about the kind of sleep we enter at bedtime. Instead it is a radical dissociation between different parts of our own being, which causes us to drift through life in daydreams. Why else would we forget why we went into the next room or where we left the car keys? If you remain skeptical about the sleep of man, just think of the amount of time you spend looking for household objects you set down a few minutes ago.

A natural reaction to this insight is indignation. After all, we go through a very complex system of behaviors, thoughts, and strategies every hour of every day. Even getting on a highway requires a remarkable coordination of perceptions, decisions, and movements.

Even so, it may not be a good idea to reject Gurdjieff's claim too fast. Some object to the idea of reincarnation on the grounds that they cannot remember their past lives, but that is hardly surprising given how little of our present lives we remember. Once I heard a radio announcer say, "And now a song from 1986." He paused for a moment and said, "I have no idea of where I was or what I was doing in 1986." People often remark how difficult it is to remember what you had for breakfast yesterday—or the color of your own front door.

Gurdjieff's pupil P.D. Ouspensky, whose *In Search of the Miraculous* is the most famous and influential presentation of Gurdjieff's thought, expresses his own experience of this idea:

> I was walking along the Troitsky street and suddenly I saw that the man who was walking towards me was *asleep*. There could be no doubt whatever about this. Although his eyes were open, he was walking along obviously immersed in dreams which ran like clouds across his face. It entered my mind that if I could look at him long enough I should see his dreams, that is, I should understand

what he was seeing in his dreams. But he passed on. After him came another also sleeping. . . . Everyone around me was asleep. It was an indubitable and distinct sensation.

As I have said, the Master Game does not call for faith. Go through your life in light of this idea of the sleep of man. Look at the people you see at your workplace, at the store, in the bus, on the subway, driving next to you on the road. Are they awake or asleep, drifting around in daydreams?

Of course, you would have to be a little bit awake yourself to investigate such a thing.

Today it is common to rant against the sleep imposed on us by the smartphone and other advanced technologies. The city of Honolulu even passed a Distracted Walking Law: "The only legal reason to look at a cell phone while in the process of crossing a street or a highway is to call 911. Any other use of a phone, tablet, or other electronic devices in a crosswalk or street can cost you."

Yet Ouspensky is describing an experience in Petrograd, Russia, in 1916, long before the people who invented the smartphone were born. It is foolish to blame technology (indeed the tendency to blame is itself a major component of the sleep of man). This kind of sleep has gone on for as long as history can tell us.

It would be all right if this sleep were merely a matter of occasional absent-mindedness. But sleep is far more pervasive and far more dangerous. Every day we hear about war, inequality, cruelty, environmental desecration, greed that is oblivious to the suffering right before its eyes. Causes are sought—economical, political, religious, spiritual, psychological—as they have been for millennia. Yet any honest evaluation would conclude that all these explanations, taken separately or together, amount to nothing.

Waking sleep is the only answer that makes sense. As Gurdjieff says, sleep is "the state in which men . . . walk the streets, write books, talk about lofty subjects, take part in politics, kill one another."

Do you agree or disagree? Look at current events. Do these seem to be the actions of sane, reasonable, compassionate people or zombies who run around imagining they are doing one thing while accomplishing the opposite? Social media, the Internet, and the usual magnets of present-day blame have changed nothing: they have merely made the problem more obvious.

If we understood the extent to which human affairs are governed by people locked into this pseudoconscious state, as Gurdjieff says, we would go mad.

The concept of sleep suggests awakening. But this awakening is not so easily accomplished. In the first place, a common first reaction to this idea is the urge to run around waking other people up. You could spend a lifetime reading and listening to pundits of all varieties telling us that we have to wake up to all sorts of issues and problems when these pundits are sleeping themselves. Their talk amounts to nothing.

Nothing can be accomplished in sleep. Therefore the first stage in the Master Game is awakening from sleep. This is not a moment of sudden illumination (though these do occur). Gurdjieff says, "Awakening is possible only for those who seek it and want it, for those who are ready to struggle with themselves and work on themselves for a very long time and very persistently in order to attain it."

Psychologist Charles Tart, building on Gurdjieff's ideas, explains why. He points out that this sleep—which he calls "consensus trance"—is so deeply rooted because it has been imparted in us since infancy. He likens it to a hypnotic trance, adding that it is much more powerful than any ordinary hypnotic state because it has been reinforced for such a long time from such an early age.

It begins with birth. A newborn comes into the world with an immature body and nervous system, totally dependent upon its parents for its very survival, as well as its happiness. There is sort of a natural consent to learn, yet the power relationship puts a strong forced quality on that consent....

The parents and the agents of the culture, the hypnotists, are relatively omniscient and omnipotent compared to the subject....

Consensus trance induction is not limited to an hour's session. It involves *years* of repeated inductions and reinforcements of previous inductions. Given the way children experience time, the cultural hypnotists have forever to work on their subjects. Further, consensus trance is intended to last for a lifetime: there are no cultural hypnotists waiting to give you a suggestion to wake up.

Notice that the "cultural hypnotists" are far more numerous and powerful than two mere parents. They consist of the whole of society—family, education, community, religion, society, nation. No one breaks these bonds with a single snap.

Awakening in turn suggests enlightenment—a word that has come to have all sorts of associations, many of them ridiculously simplistic. To some, the word evokes a cartoon image of an Eastern monk sitting cross-legged with a thought balloon containing a light bulb over his head. But according to the oldest Buddhist texts, enlightenment is complete inner freedom from the Three Poisons, which cause all suffering: desire, aversion, and avidya or obliviousness (sometimes translated as ignorance). Unless you have been entirely liberated from these three defilements, you are not an enlightened being.

There we have the answer: enlightenment is a tremendously advanced state, far beyond anything we can imagine. I have never met anyone who was close to meeting these qualifications, although I have read of some—many in the remote and legendary past—and have heard of others.

In the sense I mean above, awakening is a much simpler, more preliminary, but at least attainable stage. It can be approached from many angles, but we can start with one aspect of the sleep of humanity: the disconnection between various parts of the self.

One common way of viewing the human entity is as a trinity: the mind, the emotions, and the body. This goes back at least as far as Plato, who makes it the basis of his *Republic*, and although it is a simplistic picture, it is a useful one.

The connections between these three parts are not what they should be. Often one of them is barely in contact with the others. In some cases, the mind does not know what the body is doing. When you set down your car keys, you were thinking about your bills, how much you have to do tomorrow, how much you hate your boss—the usual things that run through our heads. Later, the mind has no idea of where the body has set down the keys because it was not paying attention. I knew a woman years ago who had this problem; she bought a fob that would beep if she clapped her hands.

The cleft between the mind and the emotions is sometimes evident in psychotherapy: when asked what they are feeling, some people do not know. They will reply by saying "I think..." or give some other mentally based response. If they are angry, sad, upset, or depressed, they barely know that they have these emotions. The many exhortations to connect the head and the heart have to do with this problem. (Folk wisdom, as manifested in the standard Hollywood script, tells us the heart is wiser than the head, but this is by no means always the case.)

The consequence of these types of dissociation is sleep, consensus trance, the hazy cloud in which we pass our lives. Awakening, then, begins with an attempt to connect these parts of the self.

Mindfulness is touted today as a solution to many problems. One version advises simply sitting down, taking a few deep breaths, relaxing, and connecting with the breath. This is based on ancient meditative practices—the Buddha taught a meditation centering on the breath—and it is valuable. If you do this, you will very likely feel better. But what happens five minutes later, when you have completely forgotten that you have done this and your mind is submerged in the same morass as before?

Mindfulness is not especially useful if it is a momentary trick, practiced once a month when you remember some directions that you heard on an audio. Something much more complete is required. So begins the real struggle with the sleep of everyday life.

Gurdjieff's answer starts with self-remembering. "*You do not remember yourselves,*" he told one group. "You do not feel *yourselves*; you are not conscious of *yourselves*. With you, 'it observes' just as 'it speaks,' 'it thinks,' 'it laughs.' You do not feel: *I* observe, *I* notice, *I* see."

This distinction may not seem obvious at first, but as soon as one starts to work with this idea, the difference between the two states is sharply clear.

Ouspensky tells of an occasion when he tried to remember himself while doing some errands. At first, distracted by the noise of a big street, he was unable to do so. But he took hold of himself and began "to experience the peace and confidence that comes after efforts of this kind."

Passing by his tobacconist, he stopped to order some cigarettes. "Two hours later I woke up in the Tavricheskaya, that is, far away. The sensation of awakening was extraordinarily vivid. I can almost say that I *came to.*"

He then realized that "while immersed in this sleep, I had continued to perform consistent and expedient actions. I left the tobacconist, called at my flat in the Liteiny, telephoned to the printers. I wrote two letters. Then again I went out of the house.... And while driving along the Tavricheskaya I began to feel a strange uneasiness, as though I had forgotten something.—*And suddenly I remembered that I had forgotten to remember myself.*"

Even remembering that you have forgotten yourself is a major step toward awakening.

What does remembering yourself mean? Say you are looking out a window. Usually your attention is completely caught by whatever is outside. In a sense, *you* have gone out the window. Self-remembering entails a kind of double attention: part of you is still looking out the window, whereas another part remains aware of you yourself inside the room. This is called *divided attention.*

Try this exercise: You are reading this book; you are paying attention to it. Now feel your feet on the floor (or wherever they happen to be); pay attention to them, sense them. Now be aware of both at the same time: your reading and your feet. See how long you can do this. Unless you are exceptional or have undergone certain kinds of training, you will probably not last for more than five seconds. Either you will feel your feet and lose the thread of what you are reading, or you will go back to reading forgetting that you even have feet.

One purpose of this practice has to do with the dissociation between the three principal centers. For a great part of our daily lives, our minds and bodies are working on different tracks. Like Ouspensky, we can perform any number of "consistent and expedient actions" while mentally absent. We are like Mr. Duffy in one of James Joyce's stories, who "lived at a little distance from his body." Self-remembering—which in this case means directing the attention of the mind to the actions and sensations of the body—is a way of forging a stronger link between the two. But it is a long and laborious process. There are no shortcuts.

Working with a connection between mind and body, what do we do with the third element: the emotions? Gurdjieff's basic practice is to refrain from the expression of negative emotions. He describes its purpose: the individual "will record with unmistakable clearness the fact that his actions, thoughts, feelings, and word are the result of external influences and that nothing comes from himself."

Take one common source of negative emotions: being cut off in traffic. This usually provokes an automatic response—honking, cursing, abusive gestures. Some people have even taken out a gun and shot the offender. Frequently these reactions take place automatically: there is no stopping them.

If you view this situation in the light of this exercise, at first you will usually notice that you had no choice in your response: your hand hit the horn before you thought of anything.

Inserting some inner space between reaction and response can be extraordinarily difficult. This is called *impulse control*. Most grown adults have mastered it to one degree or another, but that is not really consciousness: it is merely the imposition of one habitual reaction (repression) on another.

How does this exercise differ from ordinary impulse control? The latter is necessary, of course: civilized life would be impossible without it. But in this case, the emotional and physical energy contained within the reaction has no place to go: it is merely stifled. If you do this occasionally, it does no harm, but we cannot do it occasionally: there are too many day-to-day frustrations and irritations. As a result, the energy is blocked and repressed. In the long run, it takes all sorts of forms ranging from depression and anxiety to chronic disease. If the energy bursts the dam of repression, it can cause acts of violence that even the perpetrator does not understand.

Like the first exercise, struggling with negative emotions helps integrate the isolated parts of the human entity. In instances of irritation, there is usually an automatic physical reaction and an emotional correlate: honking the horn and a feeling of anger. The mind has to intervene enough to remember the practice and carry it out in the moment. This strengthens the link between these elements.

But that is not the whole of the exercise. The trick is to *feel the emotional and physical aspects of the response as fully as possible* without expressing them. If you pay attention, you will feel energy coursing through some part of your body—a kind of subtle tingling, for example, in the arms or torso. It may resemble a kind of subtle burning.

It is in fact a burning. The energy that was caught up in the response is burned up and digested by certain subtle processes in the body. You are able to use this energy rather than squandering it on a momentary explosion. It is like burning off fat. Because so much energy is usually caught up in emotional and physical tensions and responses, freeing it makes the individual feel brighter, more relaxed, and more integrated.

This is not an easy process: normally it is not taught to beginners until they have some experience with self-remembering with the body. If you try it yourself, do not be disappointed if you fail for the first few times.

Christ says, "Resist not evil: but whosoever shall smite thee on thy right cheek, turn to him the other also" (Matthew 5:39). In the light of worldly wisdom, this is utterly foolish: it is for weaklings. But think how much inner strength it must take to put this charge into practice—after all, being hit in the face is an extreme act and provokes immediate and extreme reactions.

Turning the other cheek while practicing the suggestions given above can free up and burn a great deal of negative energy. If you can do this, the one who has hit you has actually done you a favor. This is one esoteric meaning of the injunction, "Love your enemies" (Matthew 5:44).

Much of what I have said above is derived from esoteric Christianity, or what I have called *inner Christianity*. This approach takes the teachings of Christ beyond mere observances and transforms one inwardly. (For more on this subject, see my book *Inner Christianity*.)

This all has very little to do with religious observances of the familiar sort. In fact, the Gospels are full of injunctions against taking religious observances too seriously.

I am not invoking Christianity here with any hidden sectarian purpose in mind. These teachings are found in all the great world religions, and in my opinion, Christianity is no better or worse than the others. I simply use the language of Christianity because it is still the dominant religion in the English-speaking world, and even people who do not believe in it are familiar with its teachings. If I were writing for Muslims or Chinese, I could just as well use the language of their traditions. (Remember the jihad against the nafs mentioned in the previous chapter).

To stay with Christianity a little longer, Christ in the Gospels frequently mentions "the kingdom of God" or "the kingdom of heaven." But present-day religion has no idea of what he is talking about: even learned theologians will mumble vaguely about it meaning something like "divine sovereignty." The kingdom of God is about divine sovereignty—well, that is very useful.

It is peculiar: according to this religion, God the Son came down on earth once and once only and spent three years teaching. Most of his teaching has to do with this kingdom of God, and yet his most ardent disciples do not even try to discover what he was saying. The present collapse of the Christian faith has a great deal to do with failures of this kind.

Many of the parables in the Gospels speak of a master, servants, and a household. Notice that in many of these, for much of the time *the master is absent*. Here is one example:

Who then is a faithful and wise servant, whom his lord hath made ruler over his household? Blessed is that servant, whom his lord when he cometh shall find so doing. Verily I say unto you, That he shall make him ruler of all his goods. But and if that evil servant shall say in his heart, My lord delayeth his coming; And shall begin to smite his fellowservants, and to eat and drink with the drunken; The lord of that servants shall come in a day when he looketh not for him, and in an hour that he is not aware of. (Matthew 25:45–50).

The "master" here is the kingdom of God or the kingdom of heaven. It is the Supreme Self, again known to all the great traditions, who have given it their own names: Tiferet (beauty) in the Jewish Kabbalah; in the Hindu Vedic tradition, atman; nous (consciousness) in the philosophy of the ancient Greeks.

What is it?

The following practice may help illuminate this idea. You will probably do best with it if you can have someone read it to you while you do it, or you can read it aloud yourself, record it, and play it back.

Sit in a comfortable but erect position. Close your eyes. Let your attention come to the breath. Take two or three deep breaths and release them. Let the breath return to a relaxed, even state.

Now pay attention to the sensations of your body: your bottom in the seat; your feet on the floor; your back against the chair. Perhaps you can sense your hands. Focus your attention on the sensations of the body. It does not matter where or how long they last. You may find you have a sensation in one part of the body, and in the next moment sense a completely different part.

Allow yourself to continue with this for a few minutes. Connect as deeply as you can with it. You may even sense subtle currents of energy flowing through the body.

Once you have connected with the sensations of the body, now turn to the images in the mind. No doubt they have been going on ceaselessly regardless of any attempts you may make. These mental images can include pictures, memories, imaginations, emotions, ideas, complaints, grudges, worries. Watch them all as if they are flickering in front of you on a movie screen.

Again spend a few minutes watching the images come and go, releasing each one as it arises, no matter how compelling it may seem.

You have been able to observe the sensations of the body. You have been able to watch the images of the mind. So who are you?

You are not any of the things you witness, because you can watch them from a distance. What is it that witnesses all these things?

You will never be able to see this witness, because *it is that in you which sees*, far beyond the constraints of mind and body. But you cannot separate yourself from it. That is because *this is you*.

Allow yourself to rest in the presence of this witness for a few minutes. Then, as it seems appropriate, return your attention to the sensations of the body for a few minutes. When you are ready, you can open your eyes and return to your usual state of consciousness.

That witness, which you can never see but which you can never get rid of, is the Self. It is immortal, indestructible: indeed it is ultimately the only part of you that will not perish after death. Contact with it in daily life brings about freedom, liberation, joy; forgetfulness of it brings distraction and distress.

This is the kingdom of God, the kingdom of heaven: it is the master mentioned in Christ's parables. After all, you are playing the Master Game now.

The holy books of India often state clearly what the Gospels only allude to obscurely. This is from the *Mandukya Upanishad*:

The Self is the lord of all; inhabitant of the hearts of all. He is the source of all; creator and dissolver of beings. There is nothing He does not know.

He is not knowable by perception, turned inward or outward, nor by both combined. He is neither that which is known, nor that which is not known, nor is He the sum of all that might be known. He cannot be seen, grasped, bargained with. He is undefinable, unthinkable, indescribable.

The only proof of His existence is union with Him.

Much of what is obscure even in this text can be understood in the light of what we have already seen. The Self cannot be known, because *it is the knower.*

Some people are drawn to the Master Game because of an experience of illumination or transcendence. These experiences are relatively common. Generally, they are not signs of mastery. They are early clues to give the incentive to pursue the Master Game.

Once you play the Master Game, the other games of life will seem to have little importance. You probably will continue with your daily life as it is, with its relationships and responsibilities. In fact, this is usually the best approach. However tempting it may seem to run off to a monastery or become a mendicant on the streets of Benares, doing something of this sort is almost never a good idea. It is merely an attempt to escape the circumstances of your life, which are, of course, your own creation and in a sense your embodiment.

With the Master Game, you will continue to play the other games—but *as games*, not as deadly serious matters of life and death. The Master Game enables you to view all other games in their proper perspective.

The Master Game is highly individualized. No two people will play it in exactly the same way, nor should they. Sometimes the game involves psychotherapy of the conventional kind—possibly lasting for decades. In other instance, it will take you in certain directions, toward certain people or certain groups, to which you will be attracted as if by a magnet. (In fact, Gurdjieff calls this the *magnetic center*.) This process is not fool-proof: you could be attracted to a false teacher or an unscrupulous organization. If you are inwardly needy or desperate, this may even be likely. If you can be fooled, you will be.

It does not matter in the long run. Even if you spend ten or twenty years with the wrong organization and the wrong teacher, it is ultimately part of the lessons you need to learn and very likely could not have learned any other way. You may even believe you have wasted a good chunk of your life, but for the immortal and inde-structible atman, it is only a tiny blip in eternity.

All the same, some comments are in order. Most people who play the Master Game embark on a daily meditative practice. Although the rationales for these practices vary enormously, in essence, they serve as ways of reinforcing the contact of the ordinary per-sonality with the high Self, the atman.

There is an endless number of types of meditation to choose from, and the right one for you will be determined by your own needs and predilections. I would advise against organizations that charge you staggering amounts of money for learning a very simple practice that somebody else can teach you for free. In this area, monetary cost has no relation to quality, except perhaps an inverse one: the best ones usually don't charge anything.

I also have reservations about meditative practices that require major life changes in such areas as diet or sex. I would not recommend a practice that requires you to become a vegetarian unless you are already a vegetarian or want to become one anyway. Similarly for sexual strictures. You do not need to abstain from sexual activity; in fact, it is probably not a good idea. As the Catholic church has shown, for many, abstinence is not a virtue but a means of avoiding unwanted desires. If you have these, psychotherapy is usually the best approach for dealing with them. Nevertheless, I do not think that you have to have been "cured" psychotherapeutically—if that is even possible—before starting a meditative practice.

A word must be said about ethics. The Master Game has nothing to do with idiotic notions of becoming a Niezschean superman who is beyond ordinary concepts of good and evil. This attitude is a good way of ensuring that you will get nowhere.

In recent times, ethics has become needlessly complicated. The philosophy professors play speculative games: Who should be thrown overboard in a lifeboat that is too full? Would we have moral obligations to extraterrestrials? These have no relation to actuality. In fact, anyone—even a professor—thrown into one of these situations would probably behave in a way quite differently from his own well-considered conclusions. This again is part of the sleep of man.

The basic ethical obligations are simple, clear, and universal: for example, they forbid lying, cheating, stealing, killing, adultery. They are probably so widespread not because the gods came down and gave them to mankind, but because over tens of thousands of years, they have proved the best way for people to live together decently and harmoniously. You can follow the ethical teachings of Judaism, the Buddha's Eightfold Noble Path, the Sermon on the Mount, or countless other moral codes: in the end, they do not differ very much.

Moral decisions are rarely ambiguous. In almost all cases, they seem so because the people in question know the right thing to do but avoid it for the usual excuses. Sometimes when they try to squirm out of an awkward situation, their conscience will give them a sharp rap. If they have any sense, they get the message. In other cases, they refuse to pay attention, with the usual disastrous results.

Those who play the Master Game have a different attitude toward morality, even if in most cases they behave just as any ordinary decent person would. They do not hew to the rules out of fear of the policeman, the neighbors, or the wrath of the Lord. Immoral behavior is simply repellent to them: they cannot imagine doing such things, any more than they would be tempted to eat glass.

In recent decades, there has been some interest in extraordinary human functioning: unbelievable athletic achievements, paranormal powers such as clairvoyance and psychokinesis. No doubt such things are possible. But at this point it would probably be better to think of maximizing human potential in ethical terms. Adroit players of the Master Game are above conventional morality not because they can safely cast it aside but because they hold themselves to much higher standards.

There is another angle to morality. If you are to face the truth of your own sleep, this must apply to your own motives, including those for your ostensibly best and most altruistic acts. Playing the Master Game, you realize that much of the good you do is not out of care for others, but *to seem like a good person*. In the ordinary world, ethical behavior has a great deal to do with *seeming*. In cases where no one is looking, you may be acting out of a desire to seem like a good person *in your own eyes*. (The Gospels have a great deal to say about this inner hypocrisy.) Distinguishing this inner *seeming* from genuine love and compassion is a delicate, laborious, and unpleasant task. In few other areas of life do we have more propensity to lie to ourselves.

One more comment about ethics: A number of years ago, an old friend who had made a lot of money threw an enormous birthday party for himself. It was in June, so much of the event was outside, with a large canvas tent under which guests were seated.

At one point during dinner, a sudden storm came up and blew down the tent. Some people dashed out immediately. Others stood around helplessly. Still others tried to hold up the tent poles so that people could get out. It occurred to me that these reflect the three basic types of people in the world.

One question is likely to surface during the course of the Master Game: *How am I doing?* Am I making progress? Am I advancing? Am I standing still, or is the whole thing an illusion?

The Master Game is unlike the other six games in that it is not obligatory, but it is like them in that it does not finish. There is no end—at least not in the course of natural life. If there is a point of final realization, such as enlightenment, it is very far from us.

Yet wondering how one is doing in this subtle and intricate process, is unavoidable. Certainly the "peace and contentment" that Ouspensky describes in his moments of self-remembering are part of the picture. But on many other occasions, nothing will appear to be happening at all.

The responses of other people are unreliable. Friends and family may observe improvements—greater calm, less irritability, more thoughtfulness. But they are just as likely to find that your little hobby is making you colorless. You are no longer wrapped up in their games to the same extent. You are less upset when your sports teams—or your political party—loses, less exuberant when it wins. You will probably lose interest in fads, trends, and celebrities. There is often a sense of detachment from the ordinary things of life. You may seem to be colder and more impersonal, an impression that could be partly correct. After all, a short but important spiritual text published in the early twentieth century is called *The Impersonal Life*.

But that was what you wanted. You started the Master Game because you were not satisfied with the six familiar games; you sensed that there is something beyond, even if you had no idea of what. You were right.

If you have a spiritual teacher and ask him or her about your progress, you are likely to get an evasive answer. From the teacher's point of view, it is often unhelpful to give the student any clear indications. Even and especially if they are positive, they are prone to lead to the distortions of pride and self-inflation, which could take a long time to correct.

Then there are spiritual experiences. A person often starts out believing that ecstasies are the goal of the enterprise. This idea can be reinforced by early glimpses of illumination, which are fairly common. They are not signs of advancement, still less of enlightenment: they are merely mild stimuli to make you understand that there is something beyond the cavalcade of life.

Acharya Shunya, a contemporary teacher of the Advaita Vedanta tradition of India, warns against "spiritual bypassing": "Pithy statements like, 'We're all connected,' 'There is no separation,' and 'It's all one big consciousness,' make it easy enough for almost anybody to quickly imagine themselves embodying oneness, floating in a sea of nondual consciousness."

Acharya Shunya describes one woman who had been bewitched by an experience in which "the whole world took on an ethereal, dreamlike appearance, as all distinctions and dualities melted before my eyes. . . . Nothing was real, nothing was important, for all was nothing but a timeless dance of pure Consciousness."

Once this euphoria had ended, the woman felt unable to deal with the difficulties of the ordinary world. "Her short bubble of universal love and oneness burst, leaving her in an ongoing state of 'existential depression . . . aimlessness . . . and esoteric apathy.'"

Acharya Shunya insists that spiritual practice must start with purification of samsaras (mental impurities similar to the negative emotions described above); only then is one ready for higher teachings. She is right to an extent, although such depression may have different causes than is generally supposed: it comes not only from having to return to ordinary consciousness, but from deflating your belief in your own advancement. But our lives are so submerged in anxiety and depression that it is hard to fault someone for enjoying a few moments of euphoria.

This chapter began with religion. The Master Game leads some of its players to go the religious route. They may be drawn to religion, either the one they were raised in or one that is completely new: many of the leading Buddhist teachers in America today are Jews. Players of the Master Game are often drawn in this direction because they recognize that every religion has within and behind it an esoteric tradition that leads beyond belief to knowledge.

Even at this stage, religion can divert someone from the Master Game, leading back to dogmatism, bigotry, and fanaticism. "And the last state of that man is worse than the first" (Matthew 12:45).

There is, to my knowledge, only one safeguard: to participate in the outward forms of religion *while being able to go beyond them* in one's mind. All the masses, the prayers, the chants, the doctrines are veils, and it is never a good idea to stop at the veil. This is particularly true now, at a turning point of the age, when the old gods are mocked.

In the seventies, a group of Kabbalists in London created a fortune-telling game as a way of teaching people about the Kabbalistic Tree of Life. It was called *Galgal: The Master Game*. Like many such games, it has a series of cards, each with its own interpretation. There is one card called "The Veil," and its interpretation may be thought-provoking here.

When the veil had descended men revered what it covered. And as time went on it seemed to hide more and more and was revered still more. Then when it was heavy with age, young men fresh and arrogant demanded the removal of the veil, demanded to see that which was hidden. For they said that which is hidden from the people cannot be for the common good. In the thunder and lightening of indignation the veil was torn down. Nothing lay beyond. At first the young men were startled but then they laughed jubilantly at the absurd fraud that they thought they had now uncovered. And the old men grieved, cursing and blaming the young men for destroying the veil.

At some point, players of the Master Game will realize that the Self, the unseen knower, is ultimately identical in all of us (another great insight of the world's spiritual traditions). If at our core we are constituted of what has been called "the I that is we," it follows that the game cannot ultimately be played for ourselves alone. Here it goes beyond mere awakening into service. The influential esoteric author Alice Bailey speaks of "the New Group of World Servers."

It has no outer plane organisation, and those who belong to it are often totally unaware of their inclusion in any such category. They are of any class, of any nationality, of any creed or none. World betterment and human well-being at all levels mean more to them than their own individual or parochial concerns, though responsibility for these are not neglected.

At some point, players of the Master Game will realize that their aspirations cannot be complete without joining this New Group of World Servers. Their tasks, of course, are highly individualized. Today there are many doubts and fears about the future of humanity. Its survival and progress in times to come will largely be the work of this unseen but vital group.

# Afterword
## *Games and the Seven*

feel it is appropriate to say a few words about the inspiration for this book.

The original idea came from a 1968 book by Robert S. DeRopp: *The Master Game: Pathways to Higher Consciousness beyond the Drug Experience* (New York: Dell, 1968). The expression is also indebted to *Galgal: The Master Game*, which I quoted at the end of the previous chapter.

Although it is over fifty years old, DeRopp's book remains useful. His picture of the games of life influenced my thought. Here is his version, from page 13 of his book.

## Meta-games and Object Games

| Game | Aim |
|------|-----|
| Master Game | awakening |
| Religion Game | salvation |
| Science Game | knowledge |
| Art Game | beauty |
| Householder Game | raise family |
| No Game | no aim |
| Hog in Trough | wealth |
| Cock on Dunghill | fame |
| Moloch Game | glory or victory |

Although DeRopp's picture is insightful, I have redrawn the concepts along lines that I think work better. I would place his Science Game and Art Game under the creativity game; the Householder and Hog in Trough games under the survival game; and the Cock on Dunghill and Moloch games under the power game.

DeRopp's book is dated in certain ways: for example, on page 14, he writes, "Pure Hog in Trough is not considered entirely respectable in the contemporary U.S.A. and is played today with a certain moderation that would have seemed sissy to the giants of the game who savagely exploited the resources of the continent a century ago." So it may have seemed in 1968. The situation in 2023 is such as to defeat any naive belief in progress.

Even apart from changes in the contemporary scene, my arrangement seems more flexible and informative to me. It also corresponds better to other such schemata, such as Maslow's hierarchy of needs and Clare Graves' Spiral Dynamics.

My picture of the Master Game resembles DeRopp's, particularly because I have spoken at length about the ideas of G.I. Gurdjieff and P.D. Ouspensky, and DeRopp was a personal student of Ouspensky. I see no reason to fault DeRopp's presentation of their thought, but I am simply going at it from a different angle. Nor could I pretend that my presentation of Gurdjieff's and Ouspensky's views is at all comprehensive; I have simply sketched out a few basic ideas as possible entryways to the Master Game.

Nor does this book owe anything directly to *The Game of Life and How to Play It*, by Florence Scovell Shinn. Published in 1925, it is part of the American New Thought tradition. Although I had read this book, I had forgotten about it until Mitch Horowitz reminded me of it.

I also want to say something about the concept of seven. Seven is universally acknowledged as a mystical number, although the explanations frequently seem either secondary or factitious.

It would be possible to write an entire book on the symbolism of the seven, but I want to say why I believe it has been taken to be of such primal importance.

Try this: Stand up. Look above you. Look below you. Look to your front. Look to your back. Look to your left. Look to your right.

Six directions. In the middle of them, you, standing in the center.

This is the fundamental, organic structure of the human being. It is the way we perceive and orient our lives. No matter how different another human may look or act to you—no matter even if they are missing limbs—they, like you, are oriented along the same sevenfold pattern.

We have no way of knowing how an octopus or a sea urchin might conceptually construct the world. But it would probably be along very different lines.

Of course it would be possible to say more. Notice, for example, the creation myth in Genesis: six days of activity, plus one day of rest. Six directions to move in: one at the center, at rest. The *Sefer Yetzirah* ("The Book of Formation"), the oldest Kabbalistic text, is organized along similar lines. For another perspective from Jewish thought, see the treatise *On the Creation* by Philo of Alexandria, a contemporary of Christ. I have discussed this subject at greater length in my book *A Theology of Love*, particularly chapter 4.

# Notes

page 17: *Pancikarana kattam*. Kanchana Natarajan, "The Metaphysical Board Game: Avudai Akkal's *Pancikarana kattam*," *Mountain Path* 59, no. 2 (April-June 2022), 7–15.

page 19: *Maslow's hierarchy*. Saul McLeod, "Maslow's Hierarchy of Needs," Simply Psychology website, Dec. 29, 2020.

page 19: *NielsenIQ*. Genevieve Aronson, "NielsenIQ: Necessity Will Be the Strongest Consumer Driving Force of 2022," Supermarket News website, Nov. 16, 2021.

page 20: *Reiss's sixteen desires*. Steven Reiss, *Who Am I?: The Sixteen Basic Desires That Motivate Our Actions and Define Our Personalities* (New York: Berkley, 2000), 20–21, 96–98.

page 21: *Spiral Dynamics*. Don Edward Beck and Christopher C. Cowan, *Spiral Dynamics: Mastering Values, Leadership, and Change* (Malden, Mass.: Blackwell, 1996), 40.

page 24: *Leary's Game of Life*. Timothy Leary, *The Game of Life*, 2d ed. (Phoenix, Ariz.: New Falcon, 1993), 88, 96, 100, 282.

page 25: *"Scientific study of the human spirit."* Reiss, chapter 12.

page 27–28: *"The discussion can be said . . ."* Aristotle, *Nicomachean Ethics* 1094b; my translation.

page 31: *"A more stable period . . ."* Didier Fassin, *Death of a Traveller: A Counter-Investigation*, trans. Rachel Gomme (London: Polity, 2021), 73.

page 32: *"For hundreds of people . . ."* Michael J. Mooney, "Light at the End of the Tunnel," *Deseret*, Oct. 2001: 63.

page 35: *"That's everyday business here. . ."* Jack Black, *You Can't Win* (Oakland, Calif.: AK Press, 2000 [1926]), 41.

page 36: *"A basic split between shits . . ."* Burroughs, foreword to Black, 12.

page 36: *"In the months before the 1906 earthquake . . ."* Bruno Ruhland, afterword to Black, 266.

page 37: *"He had once told . . ."* Ruhland, 272.

page 37: *"Stultified and confined . . ."* Burroughs, 11.

page 38: *"I had very few glasses of wine . . ."* Black, 18.

page 41: *"He had become a partner . . ."* Anthony Trollope, *Can You Forgive Her?*, part 1, chapter 4.

page 44: *"Eleven Things Every Child Must Know about Money."* Kalen Bruce, "Eleven Things Every Child Must Know about Money (before Leaving Home)," FreedomSprout, accessed Dec. 26, 2021.

page 44: *"A woman was recently found . . ."* Michael Lesy, *Wisconsin Death Trip* (Albuquerque: University of New Mexico Press, 2000 [1973]). This edition is unpaginated.

page 45: *Definite Major Purpose.* Napoleon Hill, *The Path to Personal Power* (New York: Tarcher/Perigee, 2017 [1941]), 35.

page 46: *"Never deem any mortal . . ."* Sophocles, *Oedipus Rex*, 1529–30; my translation. Some editors have bracketed these lines as inauthentic.

page 46: *"The aim of all life is death."* Sigmund Freud, *Beyond the Pleasure Principle*, trans. James Strachey (New York: Norton, 1961), 46.

page 47: *John Mack.* See Paul Levy, *Wetiko: Healing the Mind-Virus That Plagues Our World* (Rochester, Vt.: Inner Traditions, 2021), 5.

page 47: *"Heroism, valor, and kindness . . ."* V.M. Bekhterev, *Collective Reflexology: The Complete Edition*, trans. Eugenia Lockwood and Alisa Lockwood (New Brunswick, N.J.: Transaction, 2001), 124. See also chapters 9–11.

page 50: *"Members . . . were of a peculiar kind . . ."* Claude Lévi-Strauss, *Tristes Tropiques*, trans. John and Doreen Weightman (New York: Atheneum, 1974), 290.

page 52: *Never-married people.* Wendy Wang, "The Share of Never-Married Americans Has Reached a New High," Institute for Family Studies, Sept. 9, 2020.

page 53: *"What curious feeling . . ."* Thomas Hardy, *The Return of the Native*, part 1, chapter 11.

page 56: *"Body image influences . . ."* Shirley Ojeda, "My Self-Value Used to Be Tied to My Weight. I Had to Learn to Love Myself for Who I Was," *The San Diego Union-Tribune*, Dec. 30, 2021.

page 57: *The Equation.* Richard Smoley, *Conscious Love: Insights from Mystical Christianity* (San Francisco: Jossey-Bass, 2008), 29–33.

page 58: *"Each of you . . ."* In P.D. Ouspensky, *In Search of the Miraculous: Fragments of an Unknown Teaching* (New York: Harcourt, Brace, 1949), 246.

page 59: *Jung's astrological charts.* C.G. Jung, *Synchronicity: An Acausal Connecting Principle*, trans. R.F.C. Hull (Princeton: Princeton University Press, 1973), chapter 2.

page 60: *"Couples bond when . . ."* Reiss, 143.

page 60: *"Most relationships I've been in . . ."* Iain Reid, *I'm Thinking of Ending Things* (New York: Scout Press, 2020 [2016]), 33.

page 64: *"A friend, a cliché definition . . ."* Joseph Epstein, *Friendship: An Exposé* (Boston: Houghton Mifflin, 2007), 243.

page 68: *"One brother is all brothers . . ."* A Course in Miracles, 3d ed. (Tiburon, Calif: Foundation for Inner Peace, 2007), Workbook, 161.

page 68: *"I felt myself going . . ."* Richard Maurice Bucke, *Cosmic Consciousness* (New York: Penguin Arkana, 1991 [1901]), 326–27. Emphasis in the original.

page 73: *"The power of a man . . ."* Thomas Hobbes, *Leviathan, of the Matter, Forme, Power of a Commonwealth, Ecclesiasticall and Civil*, part 1, chapter 10; in Michael Oakeshott, ed., Leviathan (Oxford: Basil Blackwell, 1957), 56; emphasis in the original.

page 79: *"By security we do not consider . . ."* Alfred Adler, *Understanding Human Nature*, trans. Walter Béran Wolfe (Cleveland: World, 1941 [1927]), 24.

page 81: *"It is always possible to recognize . . ."* P.D. Ouspensky, *The Psychology of Man's Possible Evolution* (New York: Knopf, 1972), 109.

page 82: *"In every republic . . ."* Niccolò Machiavelli, *Discourses on the First Decade of Titus Livius*, chapter 4; in Machiavelli, *The Chief Works and Others*, trans. Allan Gilbert (Durham, N.C.: Duke University Press, 1965), 1:203.

page 83: *"Love. That's why he did everything . . ."* "Citizen Kane Quotes," Rotten Tomatoes, accessed March 4, 2022.

page 83: *"For the carrying out . . ."* Leo Tolstoy, *War and Peace*, trans. Richard Pevear and Larissa Volokhonsky (New York: Vintage, 2007), 1197.

page 84: *"The primary rule is . . ."* R.G.H. Siu, *The Craft of Power* (Malabar, Fla.: Robert E. Krieger Publishing Co., 1985), 5.

page 85: *"Needs to be so prudent . . ."* Niccolò Machiavelli, *The Prince*, chapter 15; in Machiavelli, 1:58–59.

page 87: *"One definite purpose."* Napoleon Hill, *Think and Grow Rich*, ed. Arthur R. Pell (New York: Tarcher/Penguin, 2005), 3.

page 90: *"There is no other way . . ."* Machiavelli, 1:86.

page 93: *"In order that your constituency . . ."* Siu, 83.

page 94: *"If . . . Mr. Allen . . ."* Alan A. Cavaiola and Neil J. Lavender, *Toxic Coworkers: How to Deal with Dysfunctional People on the Job* (Oakland, Calif.: New Harbinger, 2000), 12–13.

page 94: *"Our own study . . ."* Cavaiola and Lavender, 3.

page 95: *"I knew I had to leave this job . . ."* Raven Ishak, "'I Suddenly Knew It Wasn't Worth It': People Are Sharing the Moment They Realized They Had to Quit Their Job (And Quit Their Manager)," Buzzfeed, Feb. 25, 2022.

page 95: "*Many things which society...*" Rodney Collin, *The Theory of Celestial Influence* (Boulder, Colo.: Shambhala, 1984 [1968]), 192.

page 97: "*Every society contains...*" Andrew M. Lobaczewski, *Political Ponerology: A Science on the Nature of Evil Adjusted for Political Purposes*, trans. Alexandra Chciuk-Celt (Grande Prairie, Alberta: Red Pill Press, 2007), 60–61.

page 97: "*Very early learn how...*" Lobaczewski, 95.

page 97: "*They begin infiltrating...*" Lobaczewski, 130–31.

page 100: "*Power-with, or influence...*" Starhawk, *Truth or Dare: Encounters with Power, Authority, and Mystery* (San Francisco: Harper San Francisco, 1987), 10.

page 100: "*Power-from-within...*" Starhawk, 10.

page 101: "*Then for the first time...*" William Styron, *The Confessions of Nat Turner* (New York: Random House, 1966), 203.

page 103: Epigraph. Quoted in Alain Daniélou, *Les quatre sens de la vie et la structure sociale de l'Inde traditionelle* (Paris: Buchet/Chastel, 1984), 131. My translation from the French.

page 104: *The pleasure of the stomach.* J.M. Rist, *Epicurus: An Introduction* (Cambridge: Cambridge University Press, 1972), 104.

page 104: "*You alone guide...*" Lucretius 1:21–24; my translation.

page 104: *Vata.* See the *Rig Veda*, 10.168.

page 105: "*In strife...*" Empedocles, fragment 21. In G.S. Kirk, J.E. Raven, and M. Schofield, *The Presocratic Philosophers*, 2d ed. (Cambridge: Cambridge University Press, 1983), 293; my translation.

page 105: "*I do not believe...*" George Parsons Lathrop, "Talks with Edison," *Harper's New Monthly Magazine*, vol. 80, no. 477 (Feb. 1890), 435.

page 106: "*Nature has placed...*" Quoted in James E. Crimmins, "Jeremy Bentham." *Stanford Encyclopedia of Philosophy*, Dec. 8, 2021.

page 106: "*The cares of political life...*" Alexis de Tocqueville, *Democracy in America*, trans. Henry Reeve (New York: Schocken, 1961), 1:293.

page 107: "Enjoyment *and* pleasure . . ." Arthur C. Brooks, "Choose Enjoyment over Pleasure," *The Atlantic* website, March 24, 2022.

page 108: "*I never enjoyed . . .*" Query to Pamela Stephenson Connolly, "Oral Sex Doesn't Appeal to Me at All. Am I Missing Out?" *The Guardian* website, March 8, 2022.

page 109: "*Far from dissuading . . .*" G. Legman, *Oragenitalism: Oral Techniques in Genital Excitation* (New York: Julian Press, 1969), 173. For etymological reasons, Legman prefers *cunnilinctus* to the usual *cunnilingus*.

page 109: "*I feel like I'm using . . .*" Jessica Stoya, "I Feel So Selfish Making My Wife Go Down on Me," Slate, May 10, 2022.

page 110: *Goonettes.* Jessica Lucas, "Meet the Goonettes: Women with Staggering Online Porn Habits," Input, accessed April 5, 2022.

page 114: "*No wine has been . . .*" Alec Waugh, *In Praise of Wine and Certain Noble Spirits* (New York: Morrow, 1959), 147.

page 115: "*Breyer's French Vanilla.*" Ling Ma, "Peking Duck," *The New Yorker*, July 11–18, 2022: 64.

page 116: *Roobs.* Roger Price, "The Great Roob Revolution," *National Lampoon* 1, no. 4 (July 1970), 5. Emphasis Price's.

page 120: "*It's only a question of . . .*" André Malraux, *Man's Fate*, trans. Haakon M. Chevalier (New York: Modern Library, 1934), 88.

page 121: "*Whosoever is found . . .*" Quoted in Matt Siegel, *The Secret History of Food: Strange but True Stories about the Origins of Everything We Eat* (New York: Ecco, 2021), 137.

page 122: "*We believe that life . . .*" Hugh M. Hefner, *The Playboy Philosophy*, chapter 8; accessed May 15, 2022.

page 123: "*The extreme sensation . . .*" Daniélou, 133–34. My translation.

page 126: "*The decline of aesthetic perfection.*" William Bell Dinsmoor, *The Architecture of Ancient Greece*, 3d ed. (New York, Norton, 1975 [1950]), 217.

page 128: "*Use the right font . . .*" Christopher Riley, *The Hollywood Reporter: The Complete and Authoritative Guide to Script*

*Format and Style*, 2d ed. (Studio City, Calif.: Michael Wiese, 2009), 1, 24.

page 129: *"Break into two."* Blake Snyder, *Save the Cat! The Last Book on Screenwriting That You'll Ever Need* (Studio City, Calif.: Michael Wiese, 2005), 78–79.

page 130: *Beats.* Snyder, 70.

page 132: *"Give me the same thing . . ."* Snyder, 21.

page 134: *"The measure is . . ."* John Milton, *Paradise Lost*, preface, "The Verse."

page 137: *"It certainly began . . ."* Aristotle, *Poetics*, 1449a, translated by I. Bywater; in Jonathan Barnes, ed., *The Complete Works of Aristotle*, 2 vols. (Princeton, N.J.: Princeton/Bollingen, 1984), 2:2319. My emphasis.

page 138: *Melissa Kirsch.* In *The New York Times*: The Morning newsletter, May 22, 2022.

page 139: *"Are you dressing . . ."* Mitch Horowitz, *Uncertain Places: Essays on Occult and Outsider Experiences* (Rochester, Vt.: Inner Traditions, 2022), 119.

page 140: *"In addition to . . ."* Horowitz, 118.

page 141: *"Suits that give . . ."* John T. Molloy's *New Dress for Success* (New York: Warner, 1988), 62

page 141: *"More doors opened . . ."* Horowitz, 122, 123. Emphasis his.

page 144: *Chuang-tzu's cook.* Brian Bruya, trans., *Zhuangzi Speaks: The Music of Nature* (Princeton, N.J.: Princeton University Press, 1992), 29–30.

page 144: *Stages of electrical expertise.* Bob Haring, "Differences between a Journeyman and a Master Electrician," Chron.com; accessed Jan. 4, 2018.

page 145: *Freemasonry.* For a fuller discussion, see Richard Smoley and Jay Kinney, *Hidden Wisdom: A Guide to the Western Inner Traditions*, 2d ed. (Wheaton, Ill.: Quest, 2006), 263–67. For a book-length introduction to Masonry, see Jay Kinney, *The Masonic Myth: Unlocking the Truth About the Symbols, the Secret Rites, and the History of Freemasonry* (San Francisco: Harper One, 2009). *Masonry* and *Freemasonry* are used more or less interchangeably.

page 145: *Hakim Bey.* Quoted in Joseph Christian Greer, "Occult Origins: Hakim Bey's Ontological Post-Anarchism," in *Anarchist Developments in Cultural Studies* 2 (2013): 176.

page 149: "*Jackson had forced . . .*" S.C. Gwynne, *Rebel Yell: The Violence, Passion, and Redemption of Stonewall Jackson* (New York: Scribner, 2014), 191.

page 150: "*I well remember . . .*" Gwynne, 522.

page 150–151: "*How every aspect . . .*" and "*Joshua's battle with the Amalekites . . .*" Gwynne, 546.

page 151: "*Let our Government . . .*" Gwynne, 515.

page 152: "*Ineffable sweetness.*" Gwynne, 551.

page 152: "'*How horrible is war.*'" Gwynne, 504.

page 153: "*The true hero . . .*" Simone Weil, *The Iliad, or the Poem of Force*, opening. On the Anarchist Library website, accessed June 29, 2022. Excerpts from this essay are taken from this site.

page 154: "*Never take counsel . . .*" Gwynne, 327.

page 154: "*We would say . . .*" Aristotle, *Nicomachean Ethics*, 1115b. This and the following quotations from Aristotle are my translations.

page 154: "*Nor would we consider . . .*" Aristotle, *Nicomachean Ethics*, 1115a.

page 155: "*Each thing is . . .*" Aristotle, *Nicomachean Ethics*, 1115b.

page 155: "*A man is properly . . .*" Aristotle, *Nicomachean Ethics*, 1115b.

page 156: *The chivalric code.* I am citing this from Charles A. Coulombe, "Soldiers of Christ," *Gnosis* 21 (fall 1991), 28. Coulombe in turn cites Leon Gautier, *Chivalry* (New York: Crescent, 1969), 19.

page 157: *Laws of Manu. The Ordinances of Manu*, trans. Arthur Coke Burnell (New Delhi: Munshiram Manoharlal, 1995 [1884]), 7:90–93; pp. 159–60. Parenthetical insertions are the translator's.

page 158: "*On the basis of . . .*" Abul Khatib, "The Need for *Jihad*," *Gnosis* 21 (fall 2021), 24.

page 159: "*Welcome to those . . .*" In Vincent J. Cornell, *Jihad*: Islam's Struggle for Truth", *Gnosis* 21 (fall 1991), 22.

page 159: "*A parachute jump ...*" Jim Morris, *The Dreaming Circus: Special Ops, LSD, and My Unlikely Path to Toltec Wisdom* (Rochester, Vt.: Inner Traditions, 2022), 74–75.

page 160: "*I believe most ...*" Morris, 116.

page 162: *Ambrose Hollingworth Redmoon.* Quotations from this article are taken from Redmoon, "No Peaceful Warriors!" *Gnosis* 21 (fall 1991), 40–44.

page 165: *R.H. Tawney.* Quoted in Alan Doherty, "R.H. Tawney: A Soldier Turned Socialist," Verso, Sept. 2, 2014.

page 167: "*Kings who ...*" *Laws of Manu* 2:89, p. 159.

page 169: Quotations from Ray Grasse are taken from "Suffering and Soul Making on the Mean Streets of Planet Earth," *Quest*, spring 2022, 35ff. The essay also appears in Grasse, *When the Stars Align: Reflections on Astrology, Life, Death, and Other Mysteries* (Chicago: Inner Eye, 2022), 80–86.

page 170: "*Presented what seems ...*" and "*I was aware ...*" Natalie Sudman, *Application of Impossible Things* (Huntsville, Ark.: Ozark Mountain Publishing, 2012), 4.

page 171: "*What seemed quite elementary ...*" and "*all of us ...*" Sudman, 27. Emphasis Sudman's.

page 176: "*The chief feature ...*" Quoted in Ouspensky, *In Search of the Miraculous*, 66.

page 177: "*I was walking ...*" Ouspensky, *Miraculous*, 265.

page 178: "*The only legal reason ...*" Website of Davis, Levin, Livingston legal firm; accessed Aug. 4, 2022.

page 179: "*The state in which ...*" In Ouspensky, *Miraculous*, 141.

page 180: "*Awakening is possible ...*" In Ouspensky, *Miraculous*, 156.

page 180: "*It begins with birth. ...*" Charles T. Tart, *Waking Up: Overcoming the Obstacles to Human Potential* (Boston: New Science Library, 1986), 91–92.

page 181: *Enlightenment.* On this subject, see John Cianciosi, "What Is Enlightenment?" *Quest: Journal of the Theosophical Society in America*, winter 2021, 26–29.

page 184: "*You do not remember yourselves.*" In Ouspensky, *Miraculous*, 117.

page 185: "*Two hours later . . .*" Ouspensky, *Miraculous*, 120–21.

page 186: *Mr. Duffy.* James Joyce, "A Painful Case," in Joyce, *Dubliners: Text, Criticism, and Notes*, Robert Schols and A. Walton Litz, eds. (New York: Viking, 1969), 108.

page 186: *Negative emotions.* In Ouspensky, *Miraculous*, 112.

page 193: "*The Self is . . .*" *The Ten Principal Upanishads*, trans. W.B. Yeats and Shree Purohit Swami (New York: Macmillan, 1937), 60.

page 202: *Acharya Shunya.* See Acharya Shunya, *Sovereign Self: Claim Your Inner Joy and Freedom with the Empowering Wisdom of the Vedas, Upanishads, and Bhagavad Gita* (Boulder, Colo.: Sounds True, 2020), 256–57.

page 203: *Galgal: The Master Game.* The original game was privately published, and few copies of it still exist. A revised version was published as *The Tree of Life Oracle*, by Cherry Gilchrist and Gila Zur (New York: Friedman/Fairfax, 202). The passage I have quoted is identical in both versions; it is on page 108 of the revised edition. *Galgal* means *wheel* in Hebrew.

page 204: "*The New Group of World Servers.*" Bailey's views are summarized in Natalie N. Banks, *The Golden Thread: The Continuity of Esoteric Teachings* (London: Lucis Press, 1963), 23.

# About the Author

Richard Smoley is an internationally acknowledged authority on the world's esoteric traditions. His books include *Inner Christianity: A Guide to the Esoteric Tradition*, *The Dice Game of Shiva: How Consciousness Creates the Universe*, and *Forbidden Faith: The Secret History of Gnosticism*. His book *Introduction to the Occult* was published by G&D Media. A graduate of Harvard and Oxford universities, he is the former editor of *Gnosis: A Journal of the Western Inner Traditions*. Currently he serves as editor of *Quest: Journal of the Theosophical Society in America*. Many of his lectures can be viewed on YouTube.

CPSIA information can be obtained
at www.ICGtesting.com
Printed in the USA
JSHW011816120223
37599JS00003B/3